AF005442

Conker Editions Ltd
22 Cosby Road
Littlethorpe
Leicester LE19 2HF
Email: books@conkereditions.co.uk
Website: www.conkereditions.co.uk
First published by Conker Editions Ltd 2025.
Text © 2025 Craig Robinson.

Craig Robinson has asserted his rights in accordance with the Copyright, Designs and Patents Act 1988 to be identified as the author of this work. All rights reserved. No part of this publication may be reproduced, stored in a retrieval system, or transmitted in any form or by any means, electronic, mechanical, photocopying, recording or otherwise, without the prior permission in writing of the publisher and the copyright owners, or as expressly permitted by law, or under terms agreed with the appropriate reprographics rights organisation. Enquiries concerning reproduction outside the terms stated here should be sent to the publishers at the UK address printed on this page.

The publisher makes no representation, express or implied, with regard to the accuracy of the information contained in this book and cannot accept any legal responsibility for any errors or omissions that may be made.

A CIP catalogue record for this book is available from the British Library.

13-digit ISBN: 978-1-0687009-0-3

Design and typesetting by Gary Silke.
Printed in the UK by Mixam.

FOOTBALL CRAZY, CORINTHIANS MAD!

The Small World of Headliners, ProStars and MicroStars Figures

CRAIG ROBINSON

FOREWORD

Corinthian figures, what can I say? The first time I set eyes on them, I knew I had to collect them. Countless journeys around London and the Home Counties ensued: who remembers Jennings of Enfield, where they would let you have a root around the stock room, and various Toys N Tuck stores in Essex? Great times. Then came the Conventions and Roadshows, including my local event, the Chelsea Day Roadshow. When one auction got way out of hand for a long-sleeve John Terry, a young lad shouted from the back, "It's only a plastic figure!"

As soon as I heard that Corinthian Marketing was going to set up a Corinthian Reseller scheme, I knew this was for me. The first series I stocked was 13. Websites were soon created: who remembers Rulermanthesecond done in Dreamweaver?! With the changing scenery of the Japanese market seemingly taking over the choice of figures, myself and another Reseller decided to launch our own Reseller Special Range, which shed light on the production process and the restraints that Corinthian had to work within.

The years passed, stock was obtained and sold, then out of the blue Corinthian announced that Series 40 would be their last ever set. 'Disappointed' was an understatement. Jump forward 30 years and we're all still collecting, though many are now down to the 'impossible-to-find' figures. The one thing always missing from the Corinthian history was a book, so it's great news that Craig has finally produced one for us all to enjoy.

Dave Rule

INTRODUCTION

Like many collectors, my Corinthian journey started one Saturday morning with a routine trip to Woolworths. Walking through the magazine aisle and past the VHS and SNES games, I resisted the pick 'n' mix sweet stand and arrived at the toy section at the back of the shop.

I can still vividly recall seeing Corinthian football figures for the very first time, the white shelf stocked with the vibrant blue packaging of the England Squad Collection. I was instantly mesmerised, buying my first Corinthian figure – Alan Shearer in England 1996 kit – never guessing that this debut purchase would start a fierce passion for collecting that has lasted over 30 years.

From that moment onwards, Corinthian football figures have remained a constant in my life. What began for myself and my brother Glenn as a way to remember our favourite players, club heroes and more obscure journeymen swiftly turned into a healthy obsession for me. Okay, at this point it is probably an addiction!

In my youth, the vast majority of my pocket money was spent on Corinthian figures and now, as a 39 year old, a percentage of my income still goes towards increasing the collection. Birthday and Christmas lists were dedicated to these little football figures. A trip to Meadowhall in

Sheffield for my 14th birthday resulted in me leaving the shopping centre with bags of Corinthians, and a grudging purchase of an Adidas zip-thru fleece. The reason for this clothing purchase is best explained by my dad on the day: "If I take you home and all you've bought is football figures, your mum will kill me!"

I hope you all remember the jingle for the MicroStars TV advert, 'Football Crazy, Chocolate Mad', which inspired the book title – and I hope you still recall the taste of the Chocolate Powerpodz. It was that cheap chocolate found in advent calendars; but that's what made it special. The only sensation to match that taste was the smell when you cut open the plastic packet that contained your MicroStars figure; many a collector still buys a sealed figure, purely to open it and inhale a trip down Memory Lane.

A key memory in my collecting journey was the moment I completed the Corinthian Headliners & Prostars collection, placing SER086 Stefan Schwarz, gifted to me by Lennart Van de Winkel, into the grandstands custom built for me by my dad. A truly special moment.

Something I've always loved about collecting, aside from the figures, is the friends you make all over the world, creating so many memories along the way, and all intrinsically attached to the figures – from Lennart's gift of Schwarz to Dave Rule offering me unreleased Master Models, and Davide Ravinale sourcing a Ravanelli Italy blister so I could include the leaflet in this book.

Personally speaking, I was always a little disappointed that there was no fully detailed and accurate record available of Corinthian football figures in book form or online. Don't get me wrong, there were some excellent websites, such as Lennart's Corinthians (created, of course, by the great Dutch collector) and Carson's Collectibles (created by Johnny Carson) but nothing that included everything. As a result, I decided to create Corinthian Archive.

Over the years the website has required numerous upgrades. The number of hours I've spent building and maintaining the site doesn't bear thinking about. It is a true labour of love, and something I'm immensely proud of. To date, the website has received over 10 million visits.

Meanwhile, my collection has grown to more than 5,000 figures, including one of every Headliners, ProStars, Club Gold, Fan Favourites, ProStars Retail, XL, MicroStars, Sharp Shooters, Key Ring and Phone Charm released by Corinthian, along with over 300 Master Models, the vast majority of which are unreleased. In addition, I have over 3,000 figures in original packaging, plus one of every SoccerStarz figure released, which to date is around 2,800.

I hope you enjoy this journey into the wonderful world of Corinthian collecting, experiencing the rare and valuable, the obscure and controversial, and even some figures you may never have seen before. Happy Collecting!

Craig

HEADLINERS 1995-1998

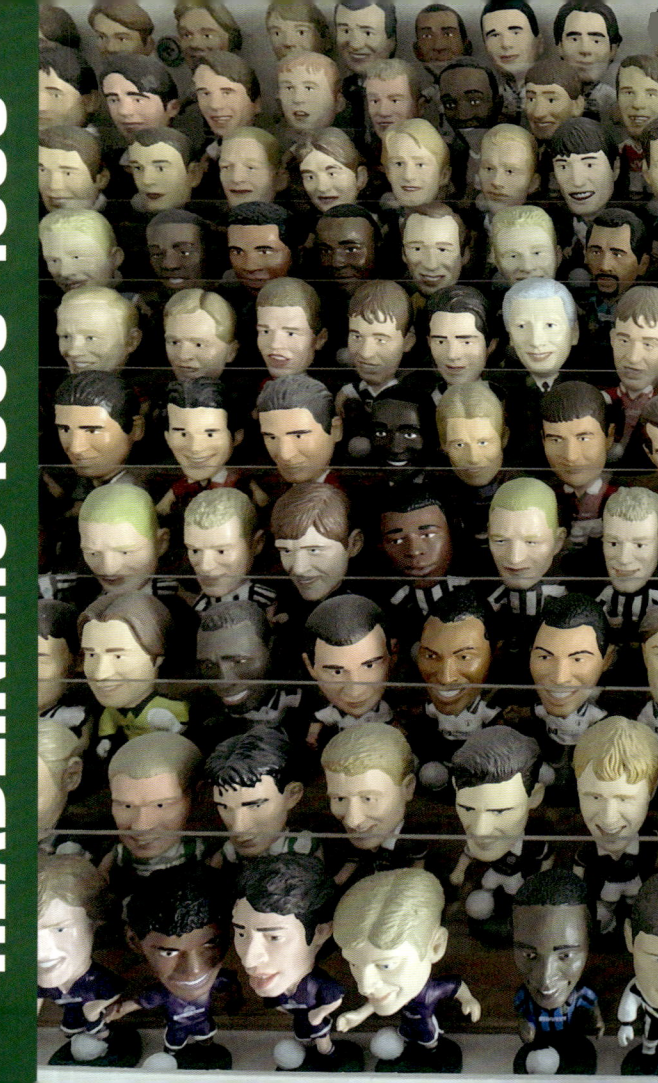

Penny Bases Cost Pounds

Prior to Corinthian figures hitting the shelves, the sales team travelled the country speaking to prospective stockists, armed with literature which detailed the forthcoming range of figures.

The sales reps also travelled with some small companions, which were initial samples of the product. These are referred to as Penny Base figures, the reason being the base was the same size as a one penny coin. Corinthian would later scale up the size of the base over concerns that the penny base size was too small and would lead to figures toppling over, or taking a dive.

The four players sculpted were Andy Cole, David Platt, Peter Beardsley and Matt Le Tissier, each figure being produced with two different paint finishes, matt and glossy. These figures provided a physical, visual aid for potential stockists, whilst also giving the sales team invaluable feedback on the figures' appearance.

The matt-finish figures bore the greater resemblance to the eventual released figures, as that style of finish allowed for finer detailing.

Corinthian never disclosed how many sets were produced but, given their role as mere sales samples, I feel the amount would have been incredibly low – a couple of dozen of each, at most.

In terms of rarity and price, it's 'Cole the Goal' who tops the charts, always the most sought after but seldom appearing for sale at around £75. None of these Penny Base are easy to find; the matt version is the more popular and sought after, and each figure can set you back £50.

Blonds Have More Fun

One of the most iconic footballing hairstyles is the bleached blond look of Paul Gascoigne. Like many football fans, one of my favourite moments is the goal Gazza scored against Scotland in Euro 96, followed by the infamous 'dentist's chair' celebration.

I'm often asked why Corinthian didn't release Gascoigne with his blond hair, the answer being that it was all down to Gazza himself. Gascoigne did approve his blond-haired figure some time before the summer tournament; however Corinthian were astonished when mere days later Gazza turned out for England with his hair dyed black.

Factory workers were then assigned the task of repainting 50,000 figures, which led to Gascoigne being held back until the second series, being replaced in the England Squad Collection first release by Matt Le Tissier.

Collectors have often wondered about the existence of a '96 blond Gazza, fuelled by the *1999 Corinthian Collector's Yearbook* which features a photo of Gascoigne himself, with his bleached-hair Master Model in front of him.

This unique item was auctioned off by Corinthian via eBay, part of eBay auction 12, which took place in September 2002. The blond-hair Gascoigne

Most players love their Corinthian figure

England 1996 Home Kit Master Model sold for £321.
 Ironically, the ever-unpredictable Gascoigne then went and re-bleached his hair for the Euro 1996 tournament. Corinthian must have been spitting when they saw the images of Gazza once again with blond hair.

Jean-Pierre Papin - What's in a Number?

March 1997 saw Corinthian release a set of 16 figures in the France national home kit. The name of the range was *Super Champions Équipe de France*, with a further four being released in June of that year.

Jean-Pierre Papin was initially released for France as part of a four-figure pack, along with Didier Deschamps, Youri Djorkaeff and Bixente Lizarazu, which hit the shelves in late March '97.

This release of Papin has him wearing the number 27, a shirt that he never actually wore! The reason behind this number error was Corinthian's production, at just the same time, of a figure of Papin for his club side Bordeaux, to be released as part of the *Super Champions 1ère Division* range – and Papin played number 27 for Bordeaux.

The production sheet for the France national home kit figure was not amended to have his squad number as nine, so it was produced instead with his Bordeaux number.

Corinthian picked up on this error after release, which explains why Papin was wearing the correct number nine by the time the single blister pack came out in June.

The hair colour is also slightly different: the number 27 version has lighter, blond hair, as opposed to the number nine version which has brown hair.

Rarity-wise, the 27 is much harder to find, as the original four pack was produced in much lower volumes than the single blister pack, though neither is by any means readily available. Value-wise, I would now expect a number nine figure to sell for around £20 and a 27 version for closer to £40.

Ciao to the Italy National Superstars

January 1998 saw the release of a set of figures in Italy national home kit, all as single blister packs. The two rarest are Roberto Baggio and Alessandro Del Piero, either one of which can easily set you back upwards of £40; however, dig a little deeper and there are a few interesting things to point out.

Fabrizio Ravanelli, nicknamed 'The White Feather', was part of this set, assigned the collector code SER089. He was initially released for Middlesbrough as part of the FAPL Collection one year earlier, in January of '97, his collector code being PL295.

Interestingly, all the Italy national kit figures of Ravanelli are base stamped the same as the Boro figure, with PL295. So no version of him actually exists correctly stamped as SER089!

It would appear Corinthian simply painted over surplus stock of the Middlesbrough version, most likely to save incurring additional costs by producing a new figure.

Also worthy of note, which has escaped many collectors over the years, is an unreleased sculpt hiding in plain sight. Look on

the back of the single blister and you'll see that between Albertini and Casiraghi is none other than Amedeo Carboni.

Carboni was released for AS Roma in March 1997, but that was an entirely different body pose. It makes you wonder how close we came to a release of Carboni in Italy home kit.

Inside the collector's information leaflet is a section titled *In Fase di Realizzazione*, which translates as 'Under Construction', where there are 11 names listed. But none of these would ever be released, and they even include some whose Master Model images have never been seen.

There are also two different versions of the collector's information file: Ravanelli has his own version, which is identifiable by the Italian badge being on a white background.

Portugal's Golden Generation

The Portuguese national team of the late '90s is often referred to as their 'Golden Generation', and with good reason when you look at the squad list. This makes their failure to qualify for the 1998 World Cup all the more perplexing; though it didn't deter Corinthian from releasing a set of 12 single-figure blister packs, headlined by Luis Figo. This was the very first release of Figo and is by far the rarest and most sought-after figure from this set.

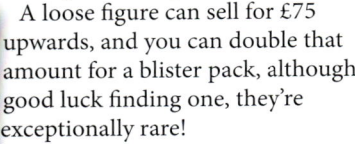

Image: Lennart Van de Winkel

A loose figure can sell for £75 upwards, and you can double that amount for a blister pack, although good luck finding one, they're exceptionally rare!

Trailing Figo in the rarity stakes are the two Pintos, João Pinto and Ricardo Sa Pinto. Loose prices are about £40-50 and blisters can go for around £75.

In true Corinthian tradition, this set does contain some anomalies, and they relate to the collector codes. Oceano Cruz was also released for Sporting Lisbon with the collector code POR001. The Portugal national figure code is POR033, and that appears on the collector card; however, the figure is base stamped POR001. José Dominguez has the collector code of POR038, but the collector card has his code incorrectly listed as POR039.

Thanks to Portugal's premier collector, Filipe Barata, for assisting with this information.

Norway and the Holy Grail

The Summer of 1998 saw Corinthian release a series of Norwegian national kit figures, distributed primarily in Norway by a company called Carlsen, and very few of these ever made their way over to the UK.

In the days before the internet and online marketplaces, it was incredibly hard to acquire these Norway figures. Collectors had to rely on Corinthian buying back some stock from the distributor, with very limited numbers being made available via official Collector Centres and through the Corinthian Collector Club.

Images: Andrew Smith

A tremendous set of 12 figures, all were released as single blister packs, with the addition of two different four packs and also a 12-figure team pack. This is seen by

many – myself included – as the 'Holy Grail' of Headliners team packs, produced in extremely low numbers. If you're ever fortunate enough to find one for sale, expect to pay anywhere in the region of £350.

Many of the figures in the set were never released by Corinthian again, players like Ståle Solbakken, Petter Rudi, Frode Grodås, Kjetil Rekdal and the bearded Erik Mykland.

The undoubted star of the set is Alfe-Inge Haaland, a figure wanted by many collectors for repaints into Nottingham Forest or Manchester City kits. Just be sure to keep him well away from any Roy Keane figures you have...

Denmark - Collectors Are Loving It

While McDonald's customers in the UK were getting a Furby or Zazu from *The Lion King* in their Happy Meal, those in Denmark were receiving a Corinthian figure. Sometimes life just isn't fair.

The figures differed from the other Headliners in that they were released on an oval base. Each figure came in a sealed clear sachet with an information card, however no collector cards were produced.

Only four of the set would ever be released by Corinthian again, these being Peter Schmeichel, Marc Rieper and the Laudrup brothers, Brian and Michael. A tricky set to complete, certain ones such as Nielsen, Hogh and Rieper are becoming much more scarce, so a full set of 12 would most likely set you back around £250.

It's interesting to note that the Laudrup brothers do not have a ball at their feet, and it has often been debated amongst collectors why this was the case. Legend has it that the figure was sculpted with a ball at his left foot, then the model was sent to the factory in China for production, but at some stage the ball broke away from the model, so it ended up being produced without. I have the Brian Laudrup tooling Master Model in my collection but can see no signs of a ball ever being present, so for now I guess the mystery remains.

Japan - Land of the Rising Nakata

Corinthian figures were becoming vastly popular all over the world, and nowhere more so than in Japan, so it was no surprise when Corinthian joined forces with Japanese company Epoch to produce a range of figures in Japan national kit.

Hidetoshi Nakata was emerging as one of the finest talents ever produced by Japan, the future Serie A star getting his first of many Corinthian releases, while fans of Dutch club Feyenoord will remember Shinji Ono.

Portsmouth fans may recall a goalkeeper by the name of Yoshikatsu Kawaguchi, who only ever only made a handful of appearances between 2001 and 2003; however, Corinthian collectors will instantly remember him for sporting perhaps the best paint job done by Corinthian. Kawaguchi is painted in the 1998 World Cup kit, which features a flame design. Corinthian and Epoch did an excellent job in replicating this iconic kit, making Kawaguchi the most desirable figure from the set. Loose, he can easily fetch £40.

The figures were released as four packs only, meaning there are four different four packs to collect in order to complete the set, and each one will cost around £50.

One final thing to note is that the set also contains football's oldest professional player, Kazuyoshi 'King Kazu' Miura, who was still playing in the 2023/24 season at the grand old age of 57.

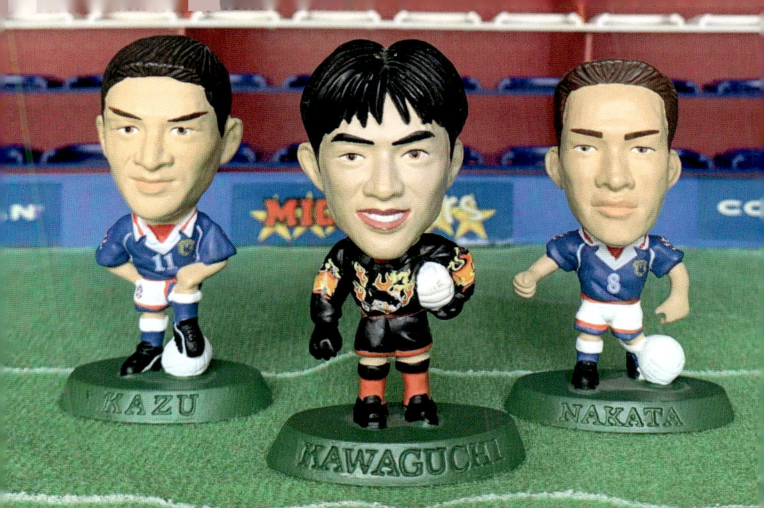
KAZU
11
KAWAGUCHI
NAKATA
8

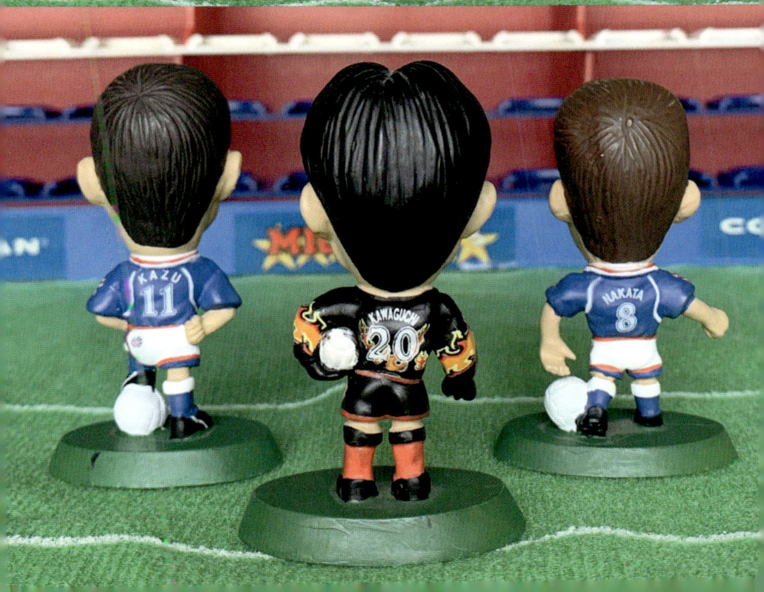
KAZU
11
KAWAGUCHI
20
NAKATA
8

Marketing Done to a Tea

World Cup fever was gripping the nation, as once again the England national team filled us full of hopes and dreams – and meanwhile Corinthian teamed up with Tetley to fill us full of tea, too.

Corinthian produced a set of 12 figures, 11 of which were included in special promotional packs of Tetley Tea. With every supermarket shelf stacked high, they would soon be coming to a playground near you.

These are undoubtedly the most common of all Corinthian figures, however as with any range there is an element of collectability in there. Gary McAllister was available as a redemption special, obtainable by sending away tokens and including a contribution towards postage and packing. You could also send away for a special 12-

figure display stand, complete with backing card. Given its status as a mail-away item, this can be more elusive, especially in sealed condition.

There was also a 12-figure team pack, which also wasn't available for general sale. Again, it had to be sent away for, which added an obstacle to acquiring one, now reflected in the value. It's certainly not competing with a Norway 12 pack, but you can expect to pay around £25 for it. As for the loose Tetley figures themselves, you would be lucky to exchange them for a single tea bag.

Something that may surprise you is the existence of three

different versions of the Tetley Tea figures. One version has them with the collector code moulded into the base, another has it stamped on in white, and the final version doesn't have any collector code at all.

I became aware of the moulded and stamped versions whilst taking the photos to include in *Football Crazy, Corinthians Mad!*, which sent me on the hunt to find them all. I could hardly comprehend that I was once again buying Tetley Tea figures.

The third version was something else I discovered while putting the book together. When I was photographing the Tetley Tea Dream Team 12 pack, Paul Ince was not quite firmly in the tray so I opened the pack, and only as I went to press him into position noticed there was no collector code under the base.

None of the figures have collector codes in the 12 pack, to which this version is exclusive. And, would you believe, there's also another variation only found in the 12 pack: the Scotland figures of Hendry and McAllister have a different shirt. The other two versions have the Scotland badge and 'UMBRO' in white, while the figures in the team pack have the badge stamped on in yellow and no branding.

Setting out to create the book, I thought there were 12 Tetley Tea figures; upon completion I now know there are

in fact 36. Even 30 years on, Corinthian can still come up with surprises.

Have fun collecting all three versions.

What a Load of Baubles

It was getting towards Christmas, I was casually scrolling eBay and suddenly these figures appeared that I'd never seen before! What I saw was the Tetley Tea figures – except now they were housed inside a plastic bauble, with string attached to the top. What's more, they weren't the regular national figures but had been repainted into Premiership club kits.

The four figures are: David Seaman – Arsenal Home 1997/98; Gianfranco Zola – Chelsea Home 1997/98; Paul Ince – Liverpool Home 1997/98; and Alan Shearer – Newcastle United Home 1997/98.

I put down my mince pie and quickly bought three full

sets. My next step was to alert fellow collectors to these curious figures, and within mere minutes the seller's stock was completely sold out.

The explanation for these figures is that Corinthian PLC

was undergoing the administration process, and during this time stock was being sold off to pay creditors. As a result, sellers and stockists were invited down to the warehouse to look over the stock.

Among the pallets of Stink Blasters, Kitty in My Pocket and Okocha Nigeria retail blisters, the reseller purchased a job lot of these Xmas baubles, not fully in the knowledge of what they were.

These figures will have been produced during the Tetley Tea promotion, but I can only guess at how they would have been released. Possibly as a special promotion towards the festive period? It's also plausible that they were just a sample product to determine the feasibility of producing Christmassy Corinthians.

I'm unsure exactly how many of each will have been produced. My assumption is Corinthian produced a few sets to use as samples, then the idea was scrapped and the product boxed up and stored away, forgotten about for over 20 years.

As you can imagine, these seldom appear for sale, as collectors who own them are reluctant to part with them. Value-wise, I feel you could expect to pay around £250 for a complete set of four.

Not a Match for Corinthian

It's often said that 'imitation is the sincerest form of flattery', however I doubt Corinthian PLC saw it quite that way when they came across this particular set of figures. Legend has it they even tried to file a lawsuit for copyright infringement.

Here we have a set of 22 football figures – they're not official Corinthian product but are of the exact same material and quality, so have often been mistaken for the real McCoy. My assumption has always been that they were manufactured in the same factory in China, as the same facial sculpts and body poses are used.

So how were these figures released, I hear you ask. Well, they were found inside a 'Match'-branded Large Lucky Bag, which was an A4-sized sealed plastic packet containing various items such as colouring sheets, crayons and sweets. And one in three bags contained one of these illicit football figures. There was even a chance to win a football strip of your choice.

The figures themselves are in a generic white kit with navy shorts, while the two goalkeepers are in an all-navy kit; but there are no names or numbers on the figures, and neither do the bases have the players' names scribed into them.

> **BIGHEADS AT AUCTION**
>
> A rare complete set of 22 Corinthian Great Britain select figures fetched at £276 at Christie's in Sept 1999. Illegally produced, unofficial figures based on the same set were destroyed after a civil action by Corinthian. However, a few survived and one sold for £322 at auction in March this year.

A superb set of figures and, although not official Corinthian, I do feel they fit perfectly into the collection.

With regards to rarity and price, they do appear on the secondary market, usually at around £5-10 each. Rio Ferdinand, Michael Owen and David Beckham are the most sought after, and could perhaps set you back £15-20.

Denilson the Record Breaker

In footballing terms, Brazil has always been highly revered when it comes to skill and prowess, often producing a wealth of talent especially in attack and forward positions.

Mention the name Denilson to football fans and they'll probably tell you about his time in Spain's La Liga at Real Betis; but bring him up with a Corinthian football figure

collector and the heart rate will increase dramatically.

Denilson first made his name playing as a winger for his hometown team, São Paulo. The summer of 1998 saw the young star make a then-world record transfer fee move to Real Betis, for £21.5 million.

Corinthian released Denilson in São Paulo kit, and it has become one of the rarest and most valuable figures in the entire collection. I assume it's so rare because after his transfer from Brazil to Spain, Corinthian scaled back production of his 'old kit' figure – coupled, of course, with the popularity of the player.

Denilson in São Paulo kit is very seldom seen for sale, a loose figure would most likely sell for £175. The collector card alone can fetch upwards of £50 and, as for a blister, you see one per decade, so pricewise it could easily trade hands for in excess of £350.

In total, Corinthian released ten figures as part of the *Brazil Futebol Collection Club*, other highlights in the set including Muller and Giovanni for Santos, which can sell for £75 and £59, respectively. We also saw the very first Corinthian release of legendary players like Cafu and Romario, the former appearing in the distinctive kit of Palmeiras.

The figures were distributed solely in Brazil by Gulliver, and during the early days of collecting it was incredibly problematic to acquire them. There were then no online stores, social media or eBay to rely on. Even Corinthian themselves struggled to re-acquire stock.

Corinthian collector 'Johnny Carson' recalls dealing with a collector in Brazil trying to secure a deal for some Denilson blister packs, all done via postal mail and fax!

The Three Ps - Pinto, Preud'Homme and... Porto's Jardel

The early part of 1998 saw Corinthian release figures of players from Portugal's Primeira Liga, with their three most famous clubs all represented. Benfica, FC Porto and Sporting Lisbon.

A tremendous trio for Benfica includes the recipient of the very first Yashin Award, Michel Preud'Homme, who won the award for his exploits in goal during the 1994 World Cup. He is joined by João Pinto and Edgar. Pricewise, it's Preud'Homme and Pinto that lead the way, each capable of fetching £50 loose and upwards of £75 if found in a good-condition blister pack.

A quartet of figures for FC Porto is headlined by Mario Jardel, who scored an incredible 130 goals in just 125 games for the club. His figure is also rare and comparable in price to the likes of João Pinto and Preud'Homme. The

other three in the set are Jorge Costa who was also released in Portugal national kit, joined by Artur Duarte and Paulinho Santos.

Four figures were also released in the famous green and white hoops of Sporting Lisbon, of which two – Oceano Cruz and Pedro Barbosa – were also available in Portugal

national kit, the set being completed by Marco Aurelio and Ivalio Iordanov. All are relatively obtainable in comparison to the others in the series, expect to pay no more than £10-15 for any of them loose and around £30 per blister pack.

It's a relatively compact Portuguese range, however there were once plans for further figures. The information file which came issued with the Portugal national figures has an image of POR021 Aloísio Pires for FC Porto, with Rui Barros, Rui Correia and Zlatko Zahovič also listed. For Benfica, Paulo Madeira and Tiago Master Models are shown, with Nuno Gomes and Calado listed. While for Sporting Lisbon the Master Model of goalkeeper Tiago is imaged, and on the list are Leandro, Beto and Simão Sabrosa. None of these figures were released and, for most, the Master Models have never been seen.

The Legend of Gijon

Sporting Gijon may not be the first team you think of when talking about football memorabilia; but in the parallel world of Corinthian collecting, I doubt any other team name has been searched as much on eBay.

Corinthian released a set of four Sporting Gijon figures as part of the *Super Champions Campeones De Futbol* series, distributed throughout Spain by Ideal.

This set consists of goalkeeper Juan Carlos Ablanedo, who spent his entire career at the club, and another product of Gijon's youth team, Alberto Tomas. The set is completed by two Russians, Yuri Nikiforov and Igor Lediakhov.

All four were released as single blister packs and there was also a four-figure pack produced, which is undoubtedly the Holy Grail of all Headliners four packs. I can count on one hand the number of times I've ever seen it for sale.

Back when I was still filling in the gaps in my collection, I came across an eBay listing that instantly caught my eye. It was the Sporting Gijon four-figure pack; however, it had been incorrectly listed as the Athletic Bilbao four pack. Could this affect its visibility to collectors? It most certainly did. I won the pack with a bid of a mere £30. I simply couldn't believe my luck. I was messaged very swiftly

afterwards by another eBay member who was from the Netherlands, none other than Lennart Van de Winkel. This was my very first communication with Lennart. I knew of him via his website which had proved an invaluable source of information, used at the time as the basis of my handwritten checklists.

Lennart congratulated me on the Gijon four pack acquisition (he had forgotten to bid, I might add) and offered me a trade: a set of four loose Gijon figures and a full complete collection of Dutch *De Spelers Collectie* figures, including the incredibly rare Winston Bogarde for Ajax. I didn't hesitate to accept, and the trade was done. And, to this day, I've never been able to acquire another Sporting Gijon four pack.

With our trip down Memory Lane complete, it's time to detail the prices of these figures. None of them are easy to acquire, the one seen most frequently for sale is Alberto

Tomas. Pricewise a loose figure would go for over £100 and a blister in the region of £150-175.

The two Russians, Nikiforov and Lediakhov, are right up there in terms of rarity and seldom appear for sale. If you're lucky enough to see them available you can expect to part with £150-200 for a loose figure, and a blister pack would cost in excess of £250.

Juan Carlos Ablanedo, the scourge of many a Corinthian collector, adorns many a wanted list. It's almost impossible to value something that never appears for sale but I would set a guide price on a loose Ablanedo at £250 and a blister would certainly be worth £350 upwards.

As for the Holy Grail four pack, I doubt anyone will ever be as fortunate as I was on eBay all those years ago. Nowadays, I would have to estimate a guide price on a Sporting Gijon four pack at around £750.

Finding Bogarde, It's a Lottery

Corinthian worked in collaboration with the Dutch lottery, Staatsloterij, to produce a range of figures featuring players from the top three clubs in the Dutch Eredivisie – perhaps needless to say, they were Ajax, Feyenoord and PSV Eindhoven.

To explain how these figures were sold and distributed, I will substitute myself off the field of play to be replaced by legendary Corinthian collector Lennart Van de Winkel.

"De Spelers Collectie figures were available wherever lottery tickets were sold, with each figure being FL6,95, which equated to around £2. The figures were released as a sealed sachet, and there was also a four-figure pack produced for each team which are incredibly rare to find, the PSV Eindhoven pack being almost impossible to track down.

Ajax had a total of 12 figures included in the range, one of which is amongst the rarest ever released by Corinthian, and this is of course Winston Bogarde!

The reason why Bogarde is so rare is that he was never officially released as part of the collection; his figure was cancelled but Corinthian did have a minuscule amount of figures in clear sachets which they made available

to collectors at the Convention.

I am proud to own a Staatsloterij sealed sachet of Bogarde. I was fortunate to acquire this item from a former employee of the Dutch lottery, who had a full set which was used for promotional purposes.

In terms of value, HOL003 Bogarde has to be on par with the likes of Andersson, Stroppa, Schwarz, Denilson and the Gijon set, selling for in excess of £200.

Bogarde aside, the rest of the Ajax figures are readily available the other 11 being the De Boer brothers Frank and Ronald, Marc Overmars, Michael Laudrup, Edwin van der Sar, Richard Witschge, Jari Litmanen, Danny Blind, Tijani Babangida, Dani and Juan.

Corinthian did list John Veldman in the 1999 Collector's Yearbook with the collector code HOL011; but this was a printing error; the figure was never released. The unreleased Master Model resides in Craig's collection, for now.

My beloved Feyenoord had 11 figures released, my personal highlight being Julio Ricardo Cruz, who scored both goals in the Champions League game against Juventus in 1997. That memory of Cruz is challenged for top place by Craig messaging me when he was recreating his website and adding ProStars Series 40. He asked for confirmation that the Cruz for Inter Milan was indeed the same Cruz as released for Feyenoord. His rationale was that the Feyenoord figure looked like an old man, instead of a 23 year old – until this moment Craig had not pieced together they were the same player!

Julio Cruz is joined by teammates Pablo Sanchez, Bernard Schuitman, Kees van Wonderen, Henk Vos, Giovanni van Bronckhorst, Jean-Paul van Gastel, Ed de Goeij, Ronald Koeman, Gaston Taument and the first release of Henrik Larsson.

Pricewise, you can pick up any of the Feyenoord figures for under £10. It's certainly worth getting the excellent first sculpt of Henrik Larsson.

PSV Eindhoven also had 11 figures released, names such as Luc Nilis, Arthur Numan, Philip Cocu, Gilles De Bilde and Wim Jonk being the most recognisable, joined by Stan Valckx, Marciano Vink, Rene Eijkelkamp, Zeljko Petrovic, Tomek Iwan and goalkeeper Ronald Waterreus. It is in fact the keeper that is the most elusive and expensive figure, for which you can expect to pay around £20.

The PSV Eindhoven four pack is exceptionally rare, I have one in my personal collection and, to date, it remains the only example I have ever seen.

Moving into the irresistible sphere of Corinthian legend, there were also rumours of a Dutch TV pundit in a raincoat being sculpted for inclusion in the range, but nobody has ever seen it, so it was only a myth... or was it?"

Effenberg and the Star Kickers

Collectors' minds often turn to the Serie A SuperStars range when there's talk of rare figures, and quite rightly so; however, no one should overlook the incredible range from the German Bundesliga, released by BanDai. The Star Kickers.

Let's kick off with Bayern Munich, 12 figures in the set consisting of top-level players like Mehmet Scholl, Giovane Élber, Lothar Matthäus, Mario Basler and legendary goalkeeper Oliver Kahn. As the figures were only released as a 12-figure team pack, I'm often asked why no single blisters or four packs were produced. The reason is simply

that Bayern requested it this way, preferring not to be selling lots of small, single, low-value items. Pricewise, obtaining a Bayern Munich 12-figure team pack will cost you between £75-100.

Borussia Dortmund had 14 figures, the most of any team in the series, and like Bayern Munich they also had a 12-figure team pack produced, which sells for a similar price. But it is the two players not included in the pack where we find the real value and rarity. Neither Knut Reinhardt nor Martin Kree are exactly household names, unless you live with a Corinthian collector, of course. But both were only released as single blister packs. Incredibly rare to find, a loose figure is £50-75 and a blister, if by some miracle you find one, could cost up to £150.

Six figures were released in the striking blue kit of 1860 Munich, all done as single blisters with a four pack also being produced, which contained Abedi Pele, Olaf Bodden, Bernhard Winkler and Jochen Kientz. Value-wise the four pack would set you back £150-200 and each single blister would be in excess of £75.

The two not released in the four pack are the rarest, those being Harald Cerny and Manfred Bender. Their figures are always in demand by those looking to complete the collection; loose, they can sell for £100 and for a blister you could pretty much double that price.

Borussia Mönchengladbach also had six figures released, all as single blisters and a four pack. The undoubted star of the entire Bundesliga Star Kickers set is Stefan Effenberg, better known for his time at Bayern Munich; but this

would be the only Corinthian figure release of the German international midfielder, which is why it is so coveted, a loose figure selling for over £100 and a single figure blister pack for over £175. Effenberg returned to Bayern Munich for the 1998/99 season, and Corinthian did intend to release him in their colours as part of a second wave of Star Kickers, however the figure was cancelled and only the Paint Master Model remains.

A special mention has to go to Christian Hochstatter. His head sculpt is enormous, rivalling that of Christian Karembeu – must be something in that first name! A final mention goes to Marcel Witeczek as, like Hochstatter, he was only released as a single blister and is seldom seen for sale. Expect to pay upwards of £75 each and over £150 for a blister.

VfB Stuttgart had five figures released and have always been viewed as the more accessible team to acquire, all except for Fredi Bobic, perhaps the second rarest figure in the Star Kickers range. And, for any Bolton Wanderers fans wondering… yes, it is *that* Fredi Bobic.

Bobic was not part of the VfB Stuttgart four-figure pack, he was only released as a single blister, another incredibly rare one to find, and value-wise he is akin to Effenberg. I don't recall ever having seen a Bolton Wanderers custom repaint, but will let you decide if that's down to the price of the figure or the fact that he only ever played 16 games for the club on loan.

Werder Bremen also had five figures released, those being Marco Bode, Bruno Labbadia, Andreas Herzog, Dieter Eilts and goalkeeper Oliver Reck. There was a four-figure pack released, with keeper Reck being omitted. Value-wise, each figure loose will be around the £50 mark and £75+ for a blister, with the four pack being in the £150-200 bracket.

Corinthian always went above and beyond to ensure the figures were as accurate as possible, and there's perhaps no better proof of this than the figure of Uwe Kamps for BMGB and Lars Ricken for Borussia Dortmund, as both figures were sculpted wearing earrings.

The figures of Effenberg, Kamps and Ricken were all depicted with earrings, something that is unique to them in the entire Corinthian collection; no other figures would ever feature any form of jewellery.

Serie A SuperStars - Gollazzo!

If you could read this with the voice of James Richardson in your head, it would really enhance the nostalgic feel. Growing up during the 1990s there was precious little live football on the TV. Premiership football was on Sky TV, which was something only the rich kids at school had access to; however, this all changed when Channel 4 introduced *Football Italia*, presented by... you know who.

Image: Lennart Van de Winkel

Saturday mornings started with cartoons and led into *Football Italia*, which was a weekly roundup of all the action from Italy's Serie A, with Richardson sitting outside a café sipping on an espresso while translating the front cover of the iconic pink newspaper *La Gazzetta dello Sport*.

Italian football was truly at its peak during this period, and Corinthian capitalised on the fact by releasing a range of football figures from Italy's Serie A. Thirteen teams are represented with a total of 50 figures released across two waves, the first in March 1997, soon to be followed by a second in July.

The first wave features a plethora of truly world-class talent. Players such as Roberto Baggio, George Weah,

Paolo Maldini, Gabriel Batistuta, Manuel Rui Costa and Alessandro Del Piero all made their Corinthian debuts.

It is from the second wave of figures that we get some of the truly rare and iconic figures, names that may seem obscure to most football fans but a mere mention of which gets Corinthian collectors' pulses racing.

The Serie A Super Seven are Domenico Morfeo for Atalanta, Kennet Andersson for Bologna, Stefan Schwarz for Fiorentina, Nicola Amoruso for Juventus, André Cruz for Napoli, Giovanni Stroppa for Udinese and Marcelo

Otero for Vicenza.

Five of these were the only releases for that particular club, and Stroppa was not even included in the information leaflet. Wave two had its own leaflet which was updated to show these new figures, even mentioning some more to be released soon, though the figure shown for Udinese was not Stroppa but, in fact, Oliver Bierhoff. Corinthian never did release Bierhoff for Udinese; collectors would have to wait until ProStars Series 2 for his initial release; only the unreleased Master Model of Bierhoff in Udinese kit remains.

The rarity order of the Serie A Super Seven has long been

a hot topic of debate amongst collectors. Like many who will be reading this, I have fond memories of the superb article on Johnny Carson's website 'Carson's Collectibles', explaining the rarity of figures. I've always concurred with him, that the rarest is Kennet Andersson, followed by Giovanni Stroppa and Stefan Schwarz.

Stefan Schwarz will always be extremely special to me, for the reason that he was the last Headliners figure I needed to complete my collection. I received an unexpected parcel from Lennart Van de Winkel, and inside was none other than Stefan Schwarz. Even though the figure is worth hundreds of pounds, Lennart sent me the figure as a gift to complete my collection.

I still recall the moment with my dad when I placed Schwarz into the display stand, honouring the promise I made to complete the Headliners collection. And I did so very much like Ric Flair after he won the 1992 Royal Rumble, 'with a tear in my eye!'

Emotional trip down Memory Lane over, let's get back to the figures, shall we? The reason behind their scarcity can be attributed to lower production volume and also to limited distribution. In many cases, I simply do not feel the figures made it to the shops.

There is a favourite, long-standing myth that there was a warehouse somewhere in Italy packed with case upon case of these rare blister packs. This was of course all mere speculation and nothing more than a rumour for over 25 years – until 2023 saw an image emerge with multiple blisters of Stroppa, Schwarz, Cruz, Amoruso, Otero and Morfeo… if not a single Kennet Andersson.

The collectors' community was abuzz with excitement. Had the long-lost warehouse stash finally been discovered? Well, not quite. The booty on show equated to around a box of each, but it was still an incredible find, helping me to complete my collector card collection and enabling many others to add these eternally sought-after blisters to their collections.

Valuing the Serie A Super Seven is no easy task, as value is so individual and personal, but I feel the prices detailed here can offer a rough price you can expect to pay for them as both loose and as a blister pack. If you're fortunate

Code	Name	Team	Loose	Blister
SER049	Domenico Morfeo	Atalanta	150	250
SER048	Kennet Andersson	Bologna	275	550
SER086	Stefan Schwarz	Fiorentina	250	500
SER047	Nicola Amoruso	Juventus	150	250
SER095	André Cruz	Napoli	150	250
SER060	Giovanni Stroppa	Udinese	250	500
SER050	Marcelo Otero	Vicenza	150	250

enough to find them for sale, that is.

Another myth to dispel here surrounds the very first release of 'El Phenomenon', Ronaldo Luís Nazário de Lima, also known as 'R9', or to those who grew up watching him, simply Ronaldo.

Ronaldo was produced in Inter Milan home kit and

assigned the collector code of SER122, however he was not released as a blister pack as part of the Serie A SuperStars range.

There was never any official reason given for this by Corinthian. My assumption has always been he was planned for release in the potential third wave but unfortunately that wave was cancelled. Given that this Ronaldo figure was part of the WorldStars set of six blisters, it makes sense that a large amount of Ronaldo figures were already produced and ready, so to make use of them Corinthian added him to that particular blister-pack release.

But the mystique does not stop there. Although a blister pack was never produced, a collector card for the SER122 figure does exist, showing an unreleased Master Model of Ronaldo, too. So where did this spring from?

I had a long-standing theory that the figure was produced in clear sachet with card and distributed by Corinthian in this format, although I had no evidence to support my case – until I had a conversation with collecting legend Frank Newton, who showed me a sealed sachet of Ronaldo SER122 with collector card.

In my personal opinion, the SER122 Ronaldo collector card Corinthian is the rarest produced. In my 30 years of collecting, I've only ever seen three.

Collecting all 50 Serie A SuperStars Headliners (51 if you include the variant of Oliveira) has always been seen as the pinnacle of Headliners collecting, and it's a club very few belong to, such is the complexity of obtaining them all.

Rarer than Schwarz?

Mention Fiorentina to any Corinthian collector and they will instinctively think of Stefan Schwarz, as everyone knows he is the rarest of the four figures for the club released as part of the Italian Superstars range. However, few collectors will be aware of the existence of a *fifth* figure for La Viola.

Brazilian forward Luís Airton Barroso 'Lulù' de Oliveira actually has a name variant, having been produced with 'OLIVEIRA' and also 'OLIVEIRA BARROS' on the back of his shirt. This is something I only discovered in 2022 on a routine scroll through eBay. When I was zooming in on a job lot auction, my eyes alit on the figure with 'OLIVEIRA BARROS' on his shirt, and instantly I knew something was

very different.

In fear that I was going mad, I quickly opened my display cabinet to check the Oliveira figure I had, and indeed the figure has 'OLIVEIRA' on the back of his shirt. I had discovered an all-new figure variant.

My next step was to search all the Oliveira figures on eBay to see if anyone was selling the variant figure. I found a couple and swiftly purchased them. My next move was to share the news with Lennart Van de Winkel, who promptly panicked and only calmed down when I informed him I had a variant figure on the way for him, too.

So far, I've been unable to precisely pin down the origin of this variant. My theory that it was released in the Super Champions International Stars sealed sachet was proved to be false, as I acquired the sachet but the figure had 'OLIVEIRA' on the back. My only assumption is that the variant was done as part of a second production run of the figure. The version with the longer name variant is by far the rarer of the two, but pricewise you will be able to pick it up for under £10.

So... is 'my' variant rarer than Schwarz, in terms of numbers made? Yes, probably. But it obviously can't rival Schwarz in terms of value and demand. Incredible to think, all these years on and Corinthian can still pull these surprises and throw up a new variant figure to hunt down.

O'Donnell and Donnelly - O, that's Why

The SFL Collection gave collectors another variant to look out for, but to explain why, we need to backtrack all the way to 1995.

For the 1995/96 SFL season, players were not assigned set squad numbers; the starting line-up wore numbers 1-11 and substitutes were assigned those from 12 onwards, which explains why the figures don't have names on the back of their shirts.

It wasn't until the 1998/99 season, and the change from the SFL (Scottish Football League) to the SPL (Scottish Premier League), that squad numbers and names on the back of shirts were first introduced – incidentally, five years after they came to the English FA Premier League.

So how does all this affect the Corinthian figures? Well, it relates to Phil O'Donnell and Simon Donnelly. January 1996 saw O'Donnell released, wearing the number seven shirt. Simon Donnelly would not be released until October 1996, also wearing number seven. Technically, this was as part of the 1996/97 season launch, although the Celtic kit was identical to 1995/96.

Also as part of the October 1996 launch of figures we saw a Celtic 12-player pack and a four-figure pack (CT4C), and in both of these multipacks the Phil O'Donnell figure is wearing the number 11 shirt. This was the shirt that he really predominantly wore, creating a new number variant for collectors.

In terms of rarity neither will prove too elusive. The number 11 is the more scarce of the two, but I would say £5 for a number seven and £10 for the 11.

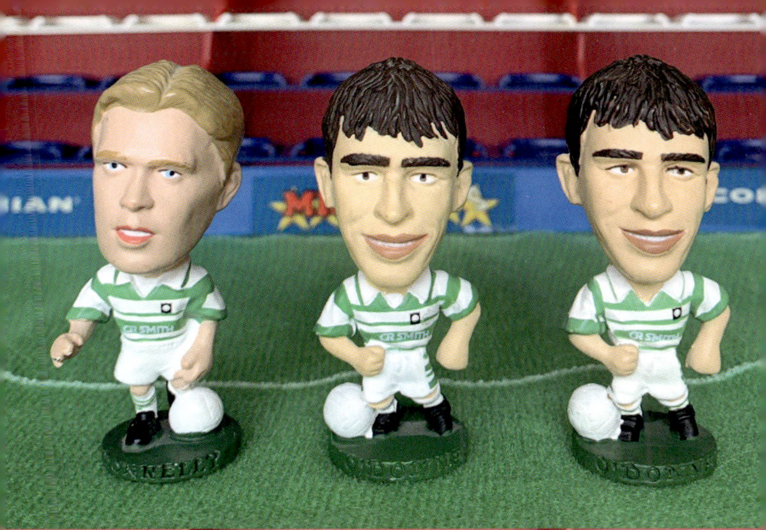
CR SMITH
CR SMITH
CR SMITH

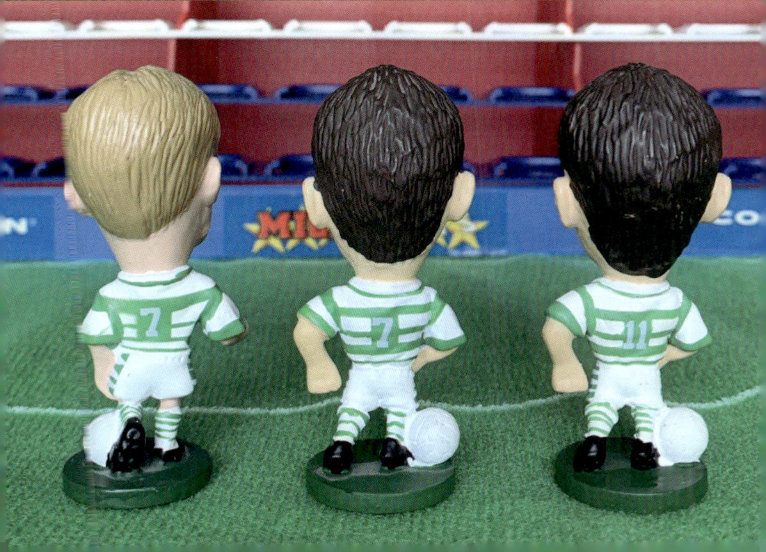
7
7
11

Owl's About These Variants?

While most of the attention for the Sheffield Wednesday figures released by Corinthian focuses on Mark Pembridge and John Sheridan, due to their rarity and value, there are actually four variants worthy of note.

Corinthian were always doing their best to ensure the figures they released were as accurate as possible, a perfect example of this being the three Wednesday figures released with two different shirt numbers, and the further addition of a hair variant.

To do this information justice, I will substitute in long-suffering Owls fan and Corinthian collecting legend, Jim Pinder.

"In 1995 most clubs still selected the starting 11 for the upcoming season and gave them the squad number accordingly, only changing this if a player left or a new player was brought in. It was only later, when replica kits were sold with numbers on, that the clubs were asked to assign squad numbers for a minimum of one season.

Sheffield Wednesday signed central defender Des Walker and assigned him the number 17. Accordingly, this figure was released by Corinthian in January 1996, but when he was selected to be a first-team regular for the new 1996/97 season he was assigned the number six, so when Corinthian re-released the figure for the new season he was brought out with his new number six on the back.

The final two figures to mention are Chris Waddle and Mark Bright. For the 1995/96 season, Bright played centre-forward alongside Hirst, and wore the number ten shirt;

however, when David Hirst got injured – just as he was lining up a move to Manchester United, as well – Wednesday moved Paul Warhurst up front, even though he was originally signed as a defender, while Bright moved back and played attacking midfield with the new squad number of eight.

Chris Waddle was the man who wore the number eight shirt from the start of the 1995/96 season, but he had to relinquish this in the circumstances and take up his new number, 15. Corinthian released Bright and Waddle with both numbers, Waddle with eight and Bright with ten for the 1995/96 season, and then when they re-released the figures for the 1996/97 season Waddle had his new number of 15 and Bright had his of eight.

The figure of Kevin Pressman was released with two different hair colours. The first is the more commonly found version and has the goalkeeper painted with dark brown hair; however, the keeper's actual hair was a light brown colour, near blond. Corinthian amended this oversight when they re-released the figure for the 1996/97 season by changing the keeper's locks to a more accurate shade. Both sculpts are exactly the same and they share the same base code of PL73.

Perhaps strangely, there is only one collector card version, which has Pressman with light brown hair, however both versions were done as single blisters."

With regards to rarity and value, finding both versions of Pressman, Walker and Bright is relatively easy and inexpensive. None of them will cost more than £15. However, this is not the case with mercurial winger Chris Waddle.

Obtaining the number eight version is straightforward and will cost no more than £10, but finding a Waddle with the shirt number 15 is exceedingly difficult, and you can expect to pay upwards of £50 for this later model.

Collecting - It's a Game of Numbers

Corinthian made every effort to keep their football figures up to date, and prime examples of their proud record can be seen in the shirt number variants found in the FAPL Collection.

Please bear in mind, this was in the days before the internet was the monster it is today, so there was no

real way for Corinthian to communicate these changes, it was up to collectors to spread the word.

Dwight Yorke was released with two different squad numbers, originally as a single blister in January 1996 for the 1995/96 season, with the squad number 18 as he was not yet an established first-team member.

Corinthian released an Aston Villa 12-figure box set in October 1996, with the figures in the same kit despite the release being for the 1996/97 season. Yorke by this time had become a first-team regular and took up the number ten shirt, prompting Corinthian to produce an updated figure accordingly.

Andy Townsend was also released with two different squad numbers, first as a single blister in January 1996 when his squad number was 11; however Tommy Johnson then moved to the club and took up the number 11, so for 1996/97 Townsend wore the number six shirt, as was reflected in the Villa 12-figure team pack.

After impressing in his debut season in the German Bundesliga for Borussia Dortmund, and on the back of a highly impressive showing at Euro 96 where he helped the Czech Republic reach the final, Patrik Berger earned himself a transfer to Liverpool.

Berger wore the number 14 shirt for the Czech Republic and, with Jan Molby no longer at Anfield, Corinthian logically expected Berger to take up the vacant number 14 shirt. Unfortunately for them, however, it was Neil Ruddock who took the 14 jersey, knocking Berger back to number 15.

The initial blister pack of Berger wearing the number 14 shirt was swiftly amended, and he was released again wearing his correct number 15 shirt. Each version is easily

identifiable by the type of blister pack: number 14 is in the standard blister pack, while the number 15 version is found in the blisters which have a 'J hook' and 'HEAD-LINERS' branding underneath the Corinthian logo.

In a similar manner, Ronny Johnsen signed for Manchester United and was given the number 19 shirt. It was not until his second season at the club that he would graduate to number five.

Corinthian released Johnsen wearing both 19 and five, the way to identify them in blister pack is by the

collector's information leaflet: the version with number 19 has 'Premier League Collector's Information Leaflet' on it, while the number five version has the word 'HEAD-LINERS' in red text below the Premier League text. Rarity-wise the number five is more elusive because it was the second production run, ordered in lower volume in anticipation of lower collector demand.

Likewise, Les Ferdinand was first released as a single blister in January 1996, having squad number nine on his back. Following the then-world record £15 million transfer of Alan Shearer from Blackburn Rovers, Les was forced to relinquish this number to Shearer, so Ferdinand took up number ten instead.

Corinthian released a 12-figure team pack in March 1996, and this time the Ferdinand figure had his new squad number of Master Model on the back of his shirt. Neither figure will prove difficult or expensive to acquire but they're both essential purchases for anyone looking to complete the collection.

Skin, Lips and Facial Hair Makeovers

As with any mass-produced item, there is always an element of variation and difference between products, and Corinthian figures are no exception to the rule.

Chris Armstrong in Tottenham Hotspur 1995/96 kit has two different variants, a second version providing an update on the initial release where the striker had been portrayed with a darker skin tone.

It is possible that the club or player asked for this change, however it's just as plausible that it merely reflected a change in factory production. What is clear is that collectors have always sought it out as a definitive variant.

A less noticeable variant but one which collectors debate over is the Andy Cole in Manchester United 1996/97 kit, where one model has more prominent lips.

Initially released in 1996/97 kit in the standard blister, Corinthian released Cole again in the 'J Hook' style blister which bears the 'HEADLINERS' branding, this version of Cole having much fuller red lips. Now, not every collector treats this as a variant, and my personal opinion is that it is simply a natural variation in production; that said, it is very cheap and easy to pick up, so is certainly worth adding to the collection.

One of the most iconic images of the Premiership era is Eric Cantona with his shirt collar rebelliously 'popped' and, rest assured, Corinthian immortalised this image by releasing a figure of Eric Cantona 'collar up'.

Corinthian's release of Cantona with a very faint beard really is one of the finest figures the company produced, 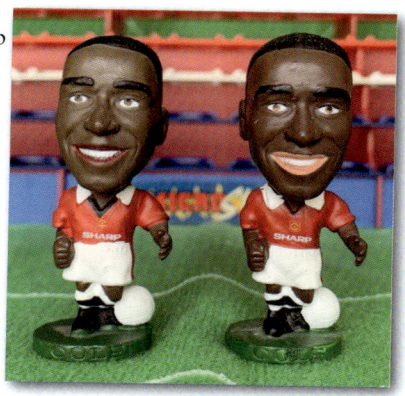 however there is also a version which has the enigmatic Frenchman with a much heavier beard, more in keeping with the Master Model image shown on the collector card.

I personally don't feel this was a predetermined change, more likely a factory variation. Nevertheless, the heavier bearded version is incredibly difficult to find, once again for the reason that it represented the second production run of the figure, which are generally manufactured in lower volumes.

Another beard variant but one which hardly gets any mention is that of Chelsea's Italian striker Gianluca Vialli. The figure in 1995/96 Chelsea kit has a very faint beard, though there is also a version where Vialli's beard is much more noticeable. The heavier bearded version is seldom seen and, like the Cantona, I feel it is nothing more

than a variation in production, which means it really is up for debate as to whether you class this as part of the collection or not. Still, when placed side by side, you can certainly see the difference. Have fun tracking down the heavier bearded versions.

Neil Ruddock, often referred to as a 'hard man in defence', was given the nickname of 'Razor' which seems ironic, looking at the two different bearded versions of him in Liverpool 1995/96 kit. One has a much lighter beard than the other, but in both cases the 'uncompromising stopper' has clearly ventured nowhere near his razor.

The final FAPL Collection variant to mention focuses on the amount of hair on Dicks. Julian Dicks for West Ham United, that is.

The more common version has him with very fair hair which is patchy in places, while another version features much darker hair that is a solid paint job with no patching.

What adds more validity and credibility to these figures being actual variants is the existence of collector cards for both versions.

The most logical explanation for this variant is that Corinthian were not sure which version to go with, so produced collector card artwork for both, using the lighter-hair version for the initial release. At a later point the factory, either by request or under their own volition, used the darker-hair artwork for the second production run, matching up the figure to the existing artwork.

The Dicks figures with darker hair are much harder to find and will prove highly elusive, that being true for both the collector card and for the figure itself.

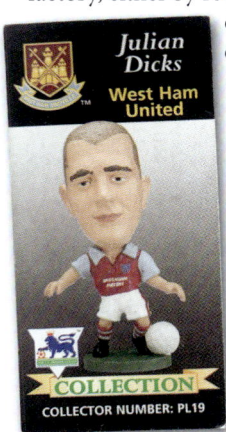

The Good, the Bad and the FAPL

Corinthian released figures for the FAPL Collection from November 1995 until February 1998, with a total of 333 different models becoming available (including shirt-number variants but not paint variants such as skin tone and facial hair). Among these figures there are, of course, many truly excellent sculpts, some absolutely shocking ones and a select number accepted as rare and expensive. On the whole, the Arsenal figures are all quite accessible, my personal favourite being Ian Wright with his gold tooth. It's worth mentioning that Lee Dixon is exclusive to the 12-figure team pack, so his loose figure can fetch £15. John Hartson and Steve Bould were not done as single blisters but were included in the 12-figure team pack and also the incredibly rare four pack AR4D, which could now set you back £75-£100.

The rarest Aston Villa figure is without doubt Alan Wright, produced in lower numbers and not included in the 12-figure team pack. He sells for £50 loose and over £100 in a blister. Wright is closely followed by Julian Joachim who fetches marginally less, with relative prices of £35 and £70.

Blackburn Rovers won the 1994/95 Premiership title, and

completing that table-topping team in Corinthian form would also require some of Jack Walker's money, as picking up a Mike Newell loose would cost £75 and a blister closer to £100. Kevin Gallacher and Jason Wilcox in a McEwan's Lager-sponsored shirt can be elusive, loose figures often fetching £25 and blisters around £35/40.

Due to their relegation, Corinthian only released four Bolton Wanderers figures, although many more were sculpted. All four are now readily available and a full set will cost less than £20.

Chelsea had not yet received their cash injection from billionaire Roman Abramovich, and his financial backing is not required to complete the Chelsea set, with no rarities amongst them. The closest we get are the three figures exclusive to the 12-figure team pack – Terry Phelan, Scott Minto and Erland Johnsen – which each often sell for £10.

Before troubles with ownership and ground descended, Coventry City were an established Premiership club. The four figures in 1995/96 kit are easy enough to acquire, though more problematic in blister and can fetch between £15-30 each. It's in the 1996/97 set where we encounter the scarcer figures, Marques Isaías and Kevin Richardson both commanding near £20 each loose and £59 for blisters. Also worthy of note is the unusually excellent sculpt of goalkeeper Steve Ogrizovic, who authenthically has his broken nose.

The Toffees provided some real sticking points for collectors, none more so than Graham Stuart, a true diamond in the collection. The reason for Stuart's rarity is his exclusive appearance in the Everton four pack EV4C. A loose figure of Stuart can easily sell for in excess of £125, and if you're fortunate enough to be offered a four pack, that can realistically sell for close to £175. Even without Stuart, the Everton figures offer up some real rarities: Dave Watson, John Ebbrell and Craig Short are all in, well, short supply. In terms of expected price, Watson leads the way with a loose figure valued at £50 and a blister almost double that, followed by Short and Ebbrell, both at £40 and £75.

Topping the list of rarity for Leeds United is Rod Wallace – £50 loose, £75 blister – and the only other Leeds figure which can prove difficult to find is Carlton Palmer, not up to the levels of Wallace but around £20 loose and over £40 in blister. The Leeds United 1996/97 set contains without doubt one of the worst figures Corinthian ever released in Lee Bowyer. Bear in mind at the time of the figure's release Bowyer was only 20 years of age, but his miniature (not very) likeness unfortunately portrays him as nearer 40.

Liverpool had a total of 39 figures released in the FAPL Collection (including both shirt-number versions of Berger) however, given the huge popularity of the club, none are particularly rare as they were all produced in high volume. The most you can expect to pay is for Michael Thomas, who commands premium prices: £15 loose and £25 for a blister. A notable mention to Dominic Matteo who was released twice, once as a blond and also with brown hair. The blond figure was a real standout in the range; it would have been interesting to see if Corinthian would have sculpted Matteo with a Faliraki tattoo, had he and Robbie Fowler not decided to go for peroxide blond hair instead.

The Manchester City side of 1995 is a far cry from the sheer brilliance of the side managed by Pep Guardiola, with Corinthian releasing just four figures, all common and valued at no more than £5 each.

Corinthian produced Manchester United figures in the highest volume, and as a result there are no

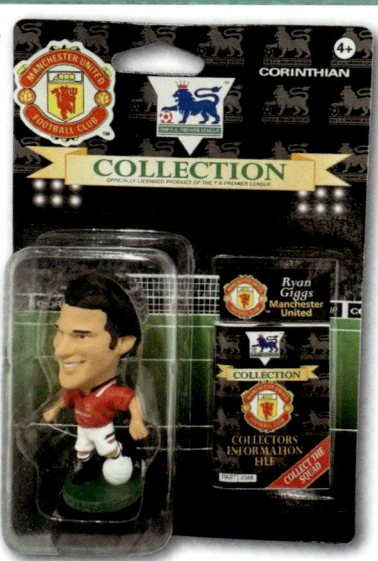

rarities amongst the set. The standout has to be Eric 'The King' Cantona with his collar up, such an iconic look immortalised in plastic. I must mention Jordi Cruyff, as this was the first time a club kit figure was released without a football included in the sculpt. and this particular body pose wasn't used for any other Headliners figure. Cruyff was released around the same time as Karel Poborksy and Ole Gunnar Solskjaer. I have vivid memories of being in Woolworths with my brother, flicking through the orange display stand of Corinthian blisters and seeing those three for the first time, unaware up to that point that they even existed. Despite our best efforts, we were unable to convince our mum to provide the additional funds required to purchase all three. My brother chose Poborsky and I went with Cruyff due to the figure's unique look, meaning the 'Baby-Faced Assassin' would have to wait for another week.

There's precious little with any rarity value among the Middlesbrough set of figures, though Bryan Robson will set you back around £15 loose and double that for a blister pack. The rest are all common, my personal favourite being Juninho, with the figure being almost life sized.

Kevin Keegan's 'Entertainers' won plaudits for their style of play but unfortunately were unable to bring any silverware home to the Geordie public. An excellent set overall, loose figures from the 1995/96 offering are common and inexpensive, but the likes of Darren Peacock, Keith Gillespie, John Beresford and Philippe Albert can be elusive in blister packs, selling for over £20 each. The Newcastle four pack NU4B is one of the rarest among those in the FAPL Collection. I have one in my personal collection and, to date, it is the only one I've ever seen. But I would love it, *love it*, if I could find another. The 1997/98 set of Newcastle United figures was a compact addition with just five figures, but it does boast a real rarity. Faustino Asprilla wasn't even listed in the *1999 Collector's Yearbook,* has always been elusive and the price has increased proportionately in recent years. A loose figure can sell for £50 and a blister in the region of £75.

Nottingham Forest had two standout figures in the 1996/97 kit, those being Andrea Silenzi and Kevin Campbell. Silenzi made just 12 appearances for Forest and is in fact the lowest-produced single blister pack in the FAPL Collection. Corinthian never disclosed how many of each figure was produced during the 1995-99 Headliners era,

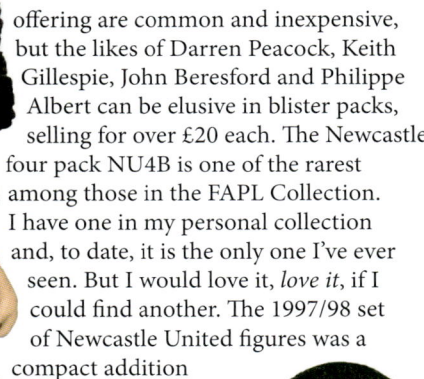

except to mention, perhaps rather cruelly, that the blister in lowest supply was Silenzi – which, as a result, can sell for over £50. Kevin Campbell has always been in high demand, usually to be repainted into a whole plethora of Arsenal kits: he's £25 loose and £75 in a blister.

Queens Park Rangers are, in certain respects, similar to Manchester City and Bolton, in that they can claim only four figures in the range, all of which are common and inexpensive, costing less than £5 each loose and £10 in blister. That's right, even with his magnificent moustache, Gary Penrice isn't a valuable commodity.

Sheffield Wednesday is one of the most difficult and financially challenging sets to complete, boasting four figure variants and two that are exceedingly rare. Obtaining both different hair versions of keeper Kevin Pressman, along with both shirt number variants for Des Walker, Mark Bright and Chris Waddle is problematic enough, especially finding

Waddle with shirt number 15; then you can add the difficulties around locating John Sheridan and Mark Pembridge. Sheridan has vastly increased in rarity value over the years, a loose figure now trading at £75 and a blister pack closer to £125. We then come to arguably one of, if not the rarest figure in the entire FAPL Collection, Mark Pembridge. Finding an example is never easy, nor is it cheap. Even loose, he can change hands for £125 and if by some miracle you encounter a blister pack, it would most likely cost you close to £200.

Southampton is another club that can boast some truly rare figures. Ken Monkou is an excellent sculpt that can fetch over £30 loose and £50 for a blister. We then have Barry Venison, Neil Heaney and Neil Shipperley who, as loose, are all over £20 with blisters along similar lines to Monkou. Manager Graeme Souness tops the lot for the Saints, a loose figure regularly selling for

£40 and a blister £65. Worth it for the moustache alone.

You can pick up the entire Tottenham Hotspur range with relative ease and minimal expense. That said, there are a few which are hard to find in blister pack, the ones whose values can top £25 each being being Sol Campbell, Andy Sinton, David Howells and Justin Edinburgh.

West Ham United is another team which will cause you headaches to complete. Acquiring an Iain Dowie alone will mean your bank balance takes a real hammering. A loose Dowie figure can fetch over £100 and a blister pack in excess of £150. The quartet of Slaven Bilic, Ilie Dumitrescu, Marc Rieper and Ian Bishop are all classed as rare, with loose figures costing in the region of £20-30 and blisters over £50 – although they seldom appear for sale.

Completing the FAPL Collection list of clubs is Wimbledon. Getting the figures loose is your best bet, the most you can expect to pay being £25 for Alan Kimble. Picking up the likes of Efan Ekoku and Alan Kimble in blister pack is never easy or cheap, either can cost anywhere from £50-75. Ekoku is one of those strange grey-area figures that you perceive to be common until you actually try to find one!

PROSTARS 1999-2008

ProStars in Forbuoys for Two Boys

By 1998 Corinthian figures had all but disappeared from shops. Bear in mind that the internet was nothing like the resource it is now, so with no presence online to provide information, we relied on publications such as *Shoot!* and *Match* magazine, which had recently carried adverts promoting the new range to be released by Corinthian, called ProStars – with Series 1 due for release early in January 1999.

I can vividly recall my brother Glenn (he was 14 at the time and myself 12) bursting through the front door exasperated, proclaiming that Corinthians were in Forbuoys, which was a newsagents in the precinct just three minutes' walk from our house. Not just any Corinthians, mind. These were the new Corinthian ProStars Series 1 Secret Sachets. A lucky dip!

The immediate standout in this tremendous new range of figures was Ronaldo in Inter Milan home kit, and we were determined to get him. We studied the poster showing all 16 figures in ProStars Series 1, and realised three had the football between the feet (Ronaldo, Bergkamp and Batistuta). We knew to be sure of getting Ronaldo we would have to feel through the sachet for the body pose.

We wrapped our Headliner figures of Bergkamp, Batistuta and Beardsley in kitchen roll inside a sandwich bag, feeling the body pose of all three figures. I was confident I'd be able to tell which sachet contained Ronaldo. So, with the high-tech experiment carried out, we grabbed our pocket money and raced down to Forbuoys.

Seeing the ProStars Series 1 Secret Sachet box on the

counter is a core memory for me. I remember the mix of excitement and nerves, thrilled to once again see the figures I love available for sale locally, but also anxious to get the Ronaldo figure.

The box was freshly opened and still contained all 16 sachets, so I began the process of feeling each one, trying to determine which had the Ronaldo. I'm sure the sales assistant must have been perplexed by my fumblings, but I was totally oblivious. I was in the zone.

Convinced I'd located the sachet with Ronaldo, we picked out another sachet at random, handed over the £4 and exited the shop. Standing outside, it was the Corinthian equivalent of the scene from *Willy Wonka* where Charlie Bucket opens his chocolate bar hoping to find the golden ticket. We carefully opened the sachet, and as I reached inside I could feel the smooth bald head. A smirk came across my face as I looked at my brother – and pulled out Ronaldo!

Our very first ProStars figure. The detail and likeness was incredible, and to this day that particular figure remains immensely special to me. Oh, and in case you were wondering who was in the other sachet we bought, it was Ronaldo's Brazilian strike partner, Romario!

The Wrong Laudrup - Oh, Brother!

Corinthian released ProStars Series 1 on 12 January 1999, giving us a blister pack series and also a secret sachet release to collect.

The Series 1 secret sachet would provide the very first mystery in the ProStars range. On the front cover is an image of a Laudrup figure in a Chelsea shirt. However, Laudrup wasn't included in this series – the Chelsea figures were Marcel Desailly and Ed de Goey – and yet more alarming is a case of mistaken identity between the Laudrup brothers.

Brian Laudrup signed for Chelsea in the summer of 1998, a move he would soon regret when he became aware of Chelsea's squad rotation system, which would mean his time at Stamford Bridge would be short lived. He made just seven appearances for the club.

Brian was originally intended to be in ProStars Series 1, but when it became apparent he would not be around when the series was released, he was pulled from the range and replaced swiftly by Ed de Goey. But sadly it was too late to change the sachet image. On top of all this, Corinthian

had mixed up the Laudrup sculpts: the figure shown on the sachet is not Brian but Michael Laudrup, which begs the question, had his figure not been cancelled, would Corinthian have released Michael Laudrup instead? Or perhaps the reason for Laudrup being pulled from the range is that Corinthian became aware of their error? We shall probably never know.

Within my personal collection are the unreleased Master Models of Michael Laudrup in Chelsea 1998/99 home and away kit. Under the bases is the sculptor's own hand-written 'Laudrup Chelsea', which only adds weight to the theory that the wrong Laudrup figure was being used.

I do wonder at what point Corinthian realised their error. That would certainly have been an awkward conversation to have in the boardroom.

Corinthian Go West - I Was the King of Wishful Thinking

The arrival of the *Corinthian ProStars Club Members' Newsletter* through the post was always exciting, reading all the latest news and of course getting to see which figures were planned for release next – my favourite ever edition being Issue 4, from February 2000.

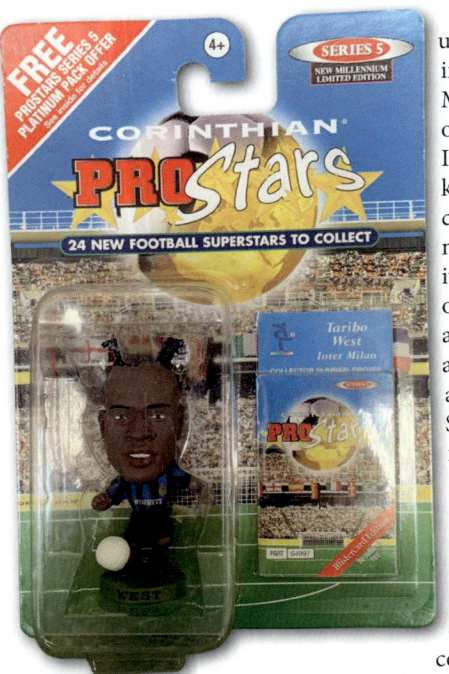

I recall picking it up off the rug and instantly seeing the Master Model image of Taribo West in Inter Milan home kit in the top right corner. Taking the newsletter from its plastic packet, I opened the cover and was greeted by a two-page spread about ProStars Series 5, which featured names like Luis Figo, Thierry Henry, Henrik Larsson, Lilian Thuram, Gianluigi Buffon – but none of these could compare with the

figure of the devil-horned Taribo West!

Unfortunately, there was not an official Corinthian Collector Centre in my town, so I had to settle for looking endlessly at the image of Taribo West. I nagged my dad relentlessly about the figure, I really was incessant.

Waking one Saturday morning to be told by my dad

that we were going on a train to Sheffield, I began wishfully thinking we would find Taribo West. Now, if this were a work of fiction, the story would end with me returning home, West blister pack in hand; however, the reality was that the Beatties store was practically sold out of all Series 5 figures. Still, I didn't return home empty handed. I may not have had Taribo West, but I did have a Beatties mail-order catalogue.

In the catalogue was a Corinthian page featuring the ProStars Series 5 figures. My shopping list was drawn up and my dad called the mail-order line. I clearly recall him saying to the operator, "Taribo West," and then looking to me mouthing the words, "sold out." My heart instantly sank, but they had most of the others on my list so the order was placed.

The parcel arrived a few days later, but we had to wait until my dad arrived home from work. The wait for quarter-past five was agony but finally he returned, taking the parcel with him upstairs as he went to get changed out of his work clothes. Another agonising wait.

Entering the front room he handed me and my brother

the parcel and, my word, there were some amazing figures inside: Figo, Larsson, Van der Sar, Ventola, amongst others, and also a Platinum pack of Nanami. As we were deciding which to open first, my dad said, 'Oh, there's one more,' and from behind his back, like some Corinthian conjuror, he pulled out a Series 5 blister pack – displaying only the back, then slowly turning it around to reveal it was Taribo West!

My face must have been a picture. I gave my dad the biggest hug, grabbing the blister pack in the process. Without a second look, I ripped it open, freeing him from the plastic prison and finally holding Taribo West in my hands.

This remains a core Corinthian memory for me; and likewise for my dad, who can now look back on the event and laugh, as it shows the lengths he would go to, helping me with my collection. So, for all these reasons, the figure of Taribo West in Inter Milan home kit from ProStars Series 5 is in my Top 5 figures, along with PL27 Ruel Fox, PL307 Shaka Hislop, SER086 Stefan Schwarz and PRO1191 Fabio Cannavaro.

The Chase Is On

Over the years, Corinthian had constantly been asked to produce a game to go with their figures, and they answered by producing the SuperClub Football game. The Match Day Edition was released in early November 2000, and to coincide with the game's release, Corinthian released their first secret sachet product since Series 2: the Squad Builder Secret Sachet. They were sold in newsagents and Collector Centres, priced at £1.99 each, and also available from Corinthian Direct, where you could get a full box, known in the trade as a CDU (Counter Display Unit) of 16 sachets, for £30.

Inside each sachet was one randomly packed figure, their collector card, a base for use in the Super Club Football game and a collector's information leaflet which detailed the figures in the sachet. In addition, there was a token, with eight of these needed to claim one of the six Series 9 Redemption figures, with only 500 of each being made.

Along with the 46 other figures, Corinthian produced something very special to help drive sales of these sachets; they made four Chaser figures, with only 500 of each Chaser figure being produced. The four figures are

David Beckham in Manchester United third kit, Michael Owen in Liverpool third kit, Ronaldo in Brazil away kit and Silvinho in Brazil home kit.

The four chaser figures were instant collector's items and have always maintained their popularity and value. Pricewise, you can expect to pay around £50 for Silvinho, £75 for Owen, near £100 for Ronaldo and in the region of £125 for Beckham. This variation in price is down to demand and popularity of the figure.

In February 2001, Corinthian announced in issue 9 of the *ProStars Club Members' Newsletter* that a case containing Squad Builder Secret Sachet Chaser figure Platinum packs and Series 9 redemption figure Platinum packs had been found in the warehouse!

These Platinum blister packs had been produced in error, with Corinthian stating they had located 23 sets and that a few sets may have already been sent out to Collector Centres before they were identified.

And so it is generally accepted by collectors that there are no more than 30 of each Chaser and Series 9 redemption Platinum packs, making them incredibly rare and viewed by many as Holy Grail pieces.

The Series 9 redemption Platinum blister packs of John Harley, David Batty, Stefen Iverson, Eyal Berkovic, Claudio Reyna and Paulo Sousa sell for anywhere in the region of £75-125; the four chaser Platinums on the other hand, should you ever find yourself in a position to them, will set you back close to £200 for Silvinho, nearer the £350/400 mark for Owen and Ronaldo, while I would expect Beckham to topple £500.

The Real Deal... Was Off

Ever since Corinthian had been producing their excellent football figures, the question the company was asked most often was, 'When are you doing figures from Real Madrid?'

The answer came in the announcement that all collectors had been praying for, in the *Corinthian ProStars Club Members' Newsletter* Issue 15, May 2002. At last, Corinthian had reached a licensing agreement with Real Madrid, which would be the jewel in their portfolio's crown.

ProStars Series 17 was all set to have four Real Madrid figures as part of the release,

Real Madrid

Real Madrid have informed Corinthian that we will *not* be able to manufacture, distribute or sell figurines of any players in the employ of Real Madrid painted in any Real Madrid strip. We are extremely disappointed that the negotiations between Real Madrid and their players, (regarding what they would receive in payment for their rights) have resulted in this negative outcome.

We have had to reject what Real Madrid considers as an acceptable payment for the players rights on the grounds that it would not be commercially viable. We would like to take this opportunity to thank all of our customers whom have expressed an interest in purchasing these figurines and thank you for your patience, as these negotiations and the issues surrounding them have been very protracted. We appreciate that there will be many of you that are disappointed but we are unable to go any further with this at the present time.

and the four Galacticos to be included were Raúl, Roberto Carlos, Zinedine Zidane and

Luis Figo, all in 2001/02 away kit.

However, the euphoria was short lived, as by the next newsletter Corinthian announced the Real Madrid licensing agreement had fallen through, due to issues over the players' image rights. The rumour has also been that the four Real Madrid figures were already packed in blisters and ready to be shipped, with the stock having to be destroyed. This is highly plausible as they appear listed on the back of the Series 17 blister pack.

Some still believe there is a warehouse in China housing these Real Madrid blister packs from Series 17, and over the years a few of the Real Madrid figures have appeared on the secondary market, though it is impossible to validate them as being genuine and authentic.

It is also possible that, as with some of the unreleased FAPL Collection figures, these also 'escaped' the factory – though, of course, they do not form part of the collection and have to be classified as unreleased, with their PRO collector codes being PRO623, PR624, PRO625 and PRO626.

It will also break collectors' hearts to know Corinthian also planned to release a Real Madrid 12-figure team

pack. The Master Models were on display at the 2002 Corinthian Convention held at Villa Park, the proposed line-up for the pack being:

PRO603	Iker Casillas
PRO604	Michel Salgado
PRO605	Roberto Carlos
PRO606	Fernando Hierro
PRO607	Iván Helguera
PRO608	Zinedine Zidane
PRO609	Steve McManaman
PRO610	Luis Figo
PRO611	Guti
PRO612	Raúl
PRO613	Fernando Morientes
PRO614	Pedro Munitis

Only the unreleased Master Models remain, and the images of the display cabinets at the Convention have become iconic amongst collectors – a tantalising glimpse of what we came so close to having. I'm in no doubt that had these Real Madrid figures been released, they would have smashed all previous ProStars sales records.

As for the Master Models themselves, most were auctioned off by Corinthian and the majority went to collectors in Japan, as their mania for all things Corinthian was at its peak during this time period.

Select 500? Select Baggio, More Like!

May 2004 saw Corinthian introduce a new series of figures, one which would prove to be their most exclusive ever. The name given to the range was the suitably portentous 'ProStars Select 500.'

As the name suggests, only 500 of each figure were produced worldwide, a number far lower than any other ProStars figure released before or since (not including Platinum packs). As a guarantee of authenticity, each figure was issued along with an individually numbered collector card, from 001 up to 500.

The figures were never made available for general sale by Corinthian, with different figures being released for the UK and Japanese markets. The UK releases were given away free for money spent with the company on other ProStars products, either at the Corinthian Conventions or via Corinthian Direct's online store or mail-order service.

This was not the case, however, with the Japanese-issued ProStars Select 500 figures, which were distributed in a variety of ways, from redemption tokens to the infamous Lucky Boxes and even a New Year's Lucky Bag!

Over a period of four years, Corinthian released a total of 46 figures in the ProStars Select 500 range, and amongst them are some of the rarest and most valuable figures in the entire collection.

During this period, Corinthian really were working at the behest of their Japanese distributor, which explains why 30 of the total of 46 of the figures are in Italian Serie A kits, as this was the European league that had become immensely popular in Japan at this time.

Despite this being a premium product, it was not immune to mistakes, as four of the figures included in the 2007 UK release have their collector cards placed the wrong way round. The four in question are Edgar Davids, Fredrik Ljungberg, Gianluigi Buffon and Arjen Robben.

Upon their release, collectors were annoyed and disappointed by this error, but Corinthian announced that they wouldn't correct their mistake by producing the figures again.

It wasn't really an option, as then there would have been 1,000 of each figure, unbefitting the Select 500 range.

The series contains five different Roberto Baggio figures, all of which are extremely rare and expensive. It's no exaggeration to say that obtaining all five could set you back in excess of £1,000.

Zidane in Juventus pink kit is another with an eye-watering price tag of £250, closely followed by Lionel Messi and Ronaldo, who is in the memorable Inter Milan third kit from the 1997/98 season.

I must admit that when Johnny Carson informed me that Hidetoshi Nakata was to feature in a Japan-released Select 500 range, I feared my collection would never be complete. Japanese Select 500 figures were already hard enough to acquire, so I dreaded to think how elusive and desirable one of Japan's sporting idols would prove. I didn't dare to even imagine Nakata's potential price.

Some time passed between the release of the Nakamura, Bergkamp and Baggio and the announcement of the Nakata figure, which led many collectors to believe that perhaps there were to be only three figures in the set instead of the customary four.

Corinthian had all but exhausted the club kits in which they could release Nakata figures; but there was still a solitary club that he had played for without being represented as a Corinthian. Nakata had gone on loan to Bologna in 2004, and despite making a meagre 17 appearances for the Italian club, it was enough for the superstar to be deemed worthy of inclusion in the ProStars Select 500 range.

I initially feared that the Japanese distributor would place Nakata inside one of their now-iconic 'Lucky Boxes' but, as it transpired, he was released in similar fashion to the Baggio, placed inside their New Year Lucky Bag, which sold for around £75.

Luckily for me, a collector friend of mine called Rikky Smith had formed a friendship with Ken Hinatra at Foot

Circle, so he was able to acquire Nakata relatively easily and for a reasonable price. Despite this fairly stress-free addition into my collection, the Nakata figure remained elusive and seldom appeared for sale. I attribute this not to a distribution error, but instead purely down to unusually

high, intensely local demand. Put simply, collectors in Japan wanted the Nakata in their collections, and they had no desire to sell to collectors in the UK, even for a hugely inflated price.

Completing the Select 500 blister pack collection is no mean feat, it is truly an elite club to be a part of. Acquiring all 46 is a monumental challenge, and I would estimate a full set to be worth around £4,500.

Cannavaro - Collection Complete

Following the success of the first Select 500 figure, PRO916 Roberto Baggio, all eyes were on Japan to see how they would distribute their next wave of the figures. The answer came in the form of the 'Lucky Box', and never has an item been so inappropriately named. Many Japanese collectors renamed it the 'Unlucky Box' – for good reason, too.

The Japanese distributors had used these Lucky Boxes before, and had found them a very effective way of shifting old stock, while at the same time driving demand for the exclusive new product which could potentially be found, in the extreme case that you were lucky enough.

Each Lucky Box contained the following:

1x ProStars blister pack
1x ProStars sachet
1x Miniatures figure (this was the name used by Japan for their MicroStars ranges).

The premise was that buying one of these boxes meant you stood a chance of finding one of the two Select 500 blister packs, of either Recoba in Venezia home kit or Cannavaro in Parma home kit. The Lucky Boxes cost about ¥525, which equated to around £5, so it was by no means an expensive product.

Due to the nature of the Lucky Boxes, it took a while for the Select 500 blisters to surface on the secondary market, but eventually they did and a few Recobas trickled out for sale. While the Recoba was not exactly commonplace, you could obtain one from Japan with the right contacts. But, meanwhile, the Cannavaro was nowhere to be seen.

The seeming non-existence of the Cannavaro infuriated collectors all over the world, with many accusing the Japanese distributors of holding the figure back to keep the Lucky Box product selling. A scandalous and plausible, if totally unproven suggestion.

To give you a further insight into how the Lucky Box really worked, you need to know how they were actually distributed. They were sold in crates of 50 Lucky Boxes to stockists, who were informed by the distributor that buying one crate guaranteed you to receive one Select 500 blister pack randomly packed into one of the 50 Lucky Boxes.

A cynical person may note that, prior to placing them on sale, the shop owners had the chance to open 50 boxes and remove the Select 500 blister pack, replacing it with a standard series release blister. How would any collector know? You would perhaps buy a few Lucky Boxes and not think anything of failing to find a rare Select 500 – certainly, no collector was going to spend £250 buying the full crate. Was the loophole ever abused in this way? It's another scandalous and plausible, if totally unproven suggestion, which again ultimately fails to explain why the Cannavaro was failing to appear, as no collector in the world had one and no contact I had in Japan was able to confirm their existence.

So, had the figure really been released, or were the suspicions of UK collectors correct, and it didn't actually exist? From what I can gather, the Japanese distributor of these figures was struggling financially and had started to reduce the price of the Lucky Boxes to shift the stock and create some cash flow. The problem with this strategy was that was that no stockist was all that interested in buying the Lucky Boxes. There was simply too little demand for them, now collectors had long given up hope of finding the Cannavaro.

I was told by a very reliable source in Japan that the distributors had reduced the price for a crate of Lucky Boxes down to £50 and were telling stockists that if they purchased five crates they were assured of receiving one Cannavaro Select 500 blister pack.

Sure enough, after I was told this a Cannavaro appeared for sale on eBay for £250. It soon sold, too, and a couple of others followed shortly after, all selling for £250. The Cannavaros soon stopped appearing for sale, though, and I gather more were sold direct to collectors in Japan, as opposed to selling them on the secondary market.

The Cannavaro is a very special figure for me personally, as it was the very last ProStars I needed to complete the entire collection. Luckily, I didn't need to spend £250 acquiring one, as I was sent mine for free.

I had phoned Simon Shaw at Corinthian PLC to discuss a couple of matters and mentioned I needed Cannavaro to complete the entire ProStars collection, asking if he would keep an eye out for one on my behalf. A week after that conversation, Simon called me again and told me he had a very interesting item sitting on his desk. It was the Cannavaro I needed, and I was left speechless.

Simon informed me the blister pack he had was the production sample, which are used for reference and promotional photographs. The figure is often hand painted by one of the UK model makers, making them of finer detail than the actual released figure, with the collector card being left unstamped, too.

I asked Simon if the figure was for sale and if so at what price. At that point I would have paid any sum of money for it. But Simon very kindly informed me that he would be sending me the blister pack free of charge, in light of the money I had previously spent on Master Models and also for the work I had put into creating the Corinthian Archive website.

For all those reasons, the Cannavaro is a very special figure to me. The last one I needed to complete the collection, and the manner in which I acquired it endears it all the more to me. I'll never forget the moment I placed him in my display stand and completed the ProStars collection.

Corinthian's 15 Ballons d'Or... or 16?

The Corinthian ProStars Ballon d'Or Series is one of the most popular series amongst collectors, and it's easy to see why when you take some of the all-time legends and release them on such a unique and interesting sculpt.

Each Corinthian figure was sculpted holding the gold Ballon d'Or trophy, wearing the suit they wore when accepting the award, presented on a special red backing card which was only used for this series of ProStars, which ran from 2001 until 2004.

Corinthian released a total of 15 figures as part of the Ballon d'Or series, however a 16th was also planned. The intention was to release it at the 2005 Corinthian Convention, with a collector code assigned in readiness, which was PRO1178.

The player scheduled as the 16th release was Andriy Shevchenko, who had also been the previous year's Ballon d'Or winner in 2004.

It's safe to say the figure was incredibly close to being released and would have been subject to cancellation very late in production.

But the reason for the figure's abandonment was not as you might have guessed, ie Corinthian wanting to avoid producing what would have been two very similar figures.

Instead, it was down to image rights relating to the Ballon d'Or trophy. As with other sporting trophies, it retains its own image rights and requires a specific licence to be used – which, from all the information I've subsequently gathered, it appears that Corinthian did not have.

By all accounts, Corinthian were contacted by the company who own the image rights to the Ballon d'Or trophy and informed that if they wished to continue using the trophy they would need to acquire the appropriate licence. If that's the case, the extra outlay might have made the figure economically unviable for Corinthian.

And so the second Shevchenko went unreleased. Only the Master Model remains.

Resellers Rule

Corinthian had their own transactional online store as well as other retail outlets selling their figures, but what really set them apart was their dedicated and enthusiastic resellers. A Corinthian reseller dealt primarily with the collector, not just carrying the latest releases but also back stock of previous releases and retired products, as well as having the contacts and resources to track down those really rare figures.

The Reseller series was done to promote the hard work and dedication shown by two resellers in particular, namely 'Corinthian Paradise' and 'Collector Mania'. The figures were not sold in any Collector Centre, store or even by Corinthian Direct, but were only available from those two official Corinthian resellers – and of course in Japan via Foot Circle (New Wave Japan), which was the official Japanese distributor.

Time for a substitution as I now come off the field to be replaced by the legendary and undisputed reseller king, Dave Rule, to explain more about the Reseller Specials.

"With regards the kit choice, there were limitations over what licences Corinthian held and of course their own plans to perhaps produce a player in that particular kit within one of their own series. The best example is from the very first series of Reseller Specials, where Antonio Careca is in Brazil away kit. He was intended to be in Brazil home kit, however Corinthian felt at the time they would themselves wish to release a Brazil home kit version as part of their very popular 'World Greats' series, so it was switched to away kit – and then Corinthian never did release a home version.

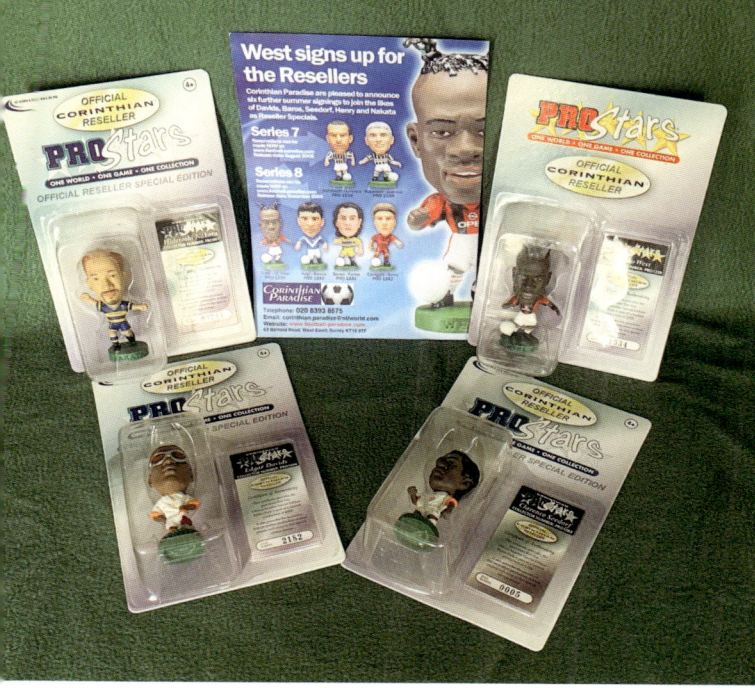

    Production volume varied significantly for the series, with a few factors contributing to this. A major factor was Corinthian insisting on a MOQ (minimum order quantity) which was set at 4,000, with that high amount ultimately leading to the range ending at Series 8. Bear in mind, at this point Corinthian were producing a lot of their own series figures with production under half of the amount they expected a reseller to commit to, and for essentially just a repainted figure, not a brand new sculpt or first-time release.

    Another factor was of course the amount of 'blanks' that

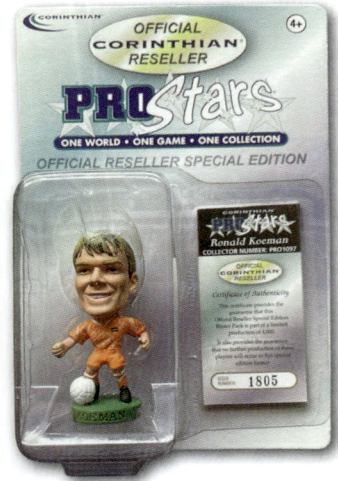

Corinthian had available. Where this really worked in the Reseller's favour was Series 4 which had Milan Baros in Czech Republic home kit and Clarence Seedorf in Holland away kit. Corinthian really wanted to use figures of players taking part in the Euro 2004 tournament, however the only two options available were Baros and Seedorf. Corinthian only had 1,062 blank Baros and 1,226 blank Seedorf available. Such low production volumes explain why those two are the rarest from the entire Reseller Specials series, and shows what the series could and perhaps should have been, a product with a much more limited-edition run.

One other complication was around the contract Corinthian had with its Japanese distributor, New Wave, as any figure that was produced as a Reseller Special, they had to be given at least 50 per cent of the stock made. There was an issue around the Nakata figure in Parma home kit, with the Resellers agreeing an amount to be made, enough to fill demand but not too much that the market was saturated, losing its long-term collectability and value – only for this to be massively increased at the request of New Wave. The Japanese distributor also received double their usually allocated stock, which explains why they made 11,767 Nakata Parma home Reseller Specials."

Arsenal Drop Four Players

In early 2007 Corinthian released a set of eight Arsenal figures, all on a specially designed, club-specific backing card, with the vast majority of the stock going to the Arsenal club shop.

It's a tremendous set which provided the only ProStars release of Gaël Clichy, a figure notoriously difficult to find. It can sell for £25 in blister pack, and is actually easier to find in the Platinum blister packs than the regular release blisters.

Corinthian's original plan was to release them as part of a 12-figure team pack; of the four that were cancelled, two would have been first-time releases.

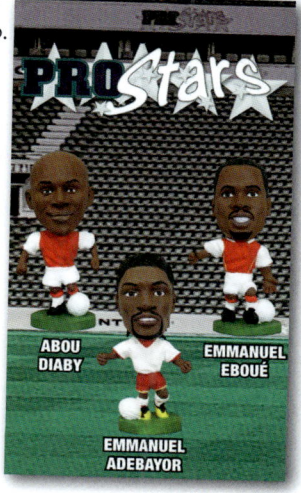

All four were assigned collector codes: PRO1674 Jens Lehman in 2006/07 goalkeeper kit, joined by PRO1685 Emmanuel Adebayor in the 2006/07 away kit. The remaining two would have been in home kit, those being first-time releases of PRO1678 Emanuel Eboué and PRO1682 Abou Diaby.

The reason for the team pack being cancelled was never officially detailed by Corinthian, but my assumption is that the sculpts didn't receive the required approval.

As for the unreleased Master Models, Diaby, Eboué and Adebayor were sold to Japanese seller Madbooth. I am unsure as to what happened to the Lehman paint master.

Aztec a Look at These Mexico Figures

Corinthian enjoyed success with their range of MicroStars released in Mexico, so in the summer of 2006 they released a set of eight ProStars figures in Mexico home kit, which were exclusively sold and distributed in the country itself. Corinthian made no mention of the figures' existence in any of the newsletters issued to Collector Club members: to many of us, there were just eight collector code gaps in our collections, and for a while it was assumed they were never released.

The set of eight is superbly put together, from the bright and vibrant Aztec-style blister pack to the quality of the sculpts, five of which we never saw again. It all adds up to make this series one of my favourites Corinthian ever released.

There are eight figures in the set, six of which were first-time sculpts. Jared Borgetti was first released in Bolton kit as part of ProStars Series 32 and then in Mexico home kit as part of the 2006 Convention series. Rafael Márquez had been released a few times for Barcelona prior to this, the sculpt used here being the second one, also used in the Barcelona Champions of Europe 2006 team pack.

Giovanni dos Santos got his first ever ProStars release,

the only other being in the Barcelona home kit as part of ProStars Classics Series 3. The other five are first-time sculpts which would never be released by Corinthian again, these being Oswaldo Sánchez, Carlos Vela, Pável Pardo, Carlos Salcido and Cuauhtémoc Blanco.

The figures have always been rare, given their country of release and the fact it was never possible to order them directly from Corinthian. Goalkeeper Oswaldo Sánchez leads the way in terms of value: a blister pack can comfortably fetch £50, with forward Cuauhtémoc Blanco fetching around £40, and the trio of Salcido, Pardo and Vela close behind at £30.

The prices have shot up over the years as the figures have become increasingly hard to obtain. In the summer of 2008 I imported ten full sets to help the collector community, although you can still really struggle to find a single set for sale, with just 3,186 blisters being made of each.

Craques da Bola

In December 2007, Corinthian released a series of ten ProStars figures in Brazil, called *Craques da Bola,* which translates from Portuguese as 'Ball Stars'. It featured the players in their club kits, the figures being sold throughout Brazil by DTC (Direct Toys Company).

This series proved to be very controversial due to the complexity and problems collectors outside Brazil encountered when trying to acquire the figures. For a long time it was widely accepted that not all ten were released; it was assumed by collectors that just two had been released – Rooney and Ronaldinho – as they were the only ones that had been sighted. Even Corinthian themselves could not confirm the existence of the full set of Master Models.

I used to scour Mercado Livre, which is essentially a

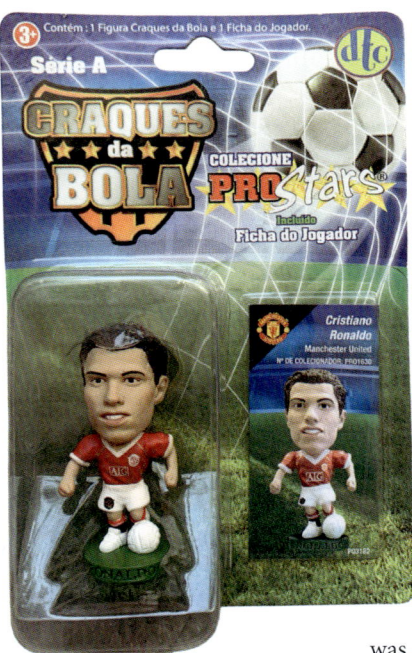

South American version of eBay, in the vain hope of finding the elusive eight figures. My hours of endless trawling and persistence finally paid off when I encountered a seller who was advertising not just one or two figures, but full sets.

I enlisted the help of a friend in Brazil who was able to communicate with the seller. It turns out the seller owned a discount warehouse and did in fact have 20 full sets available. My friend asked me how many sets I wanted, and my instant reply was, "All of them!"

After some negotiation we agreed on a price which was £5 per blister, so £50 for a full set; however, there was then the cost of importing them which, as you can imagine, was rather eye watering. The wait for them to arrive was agony, as were the extortionate customs fees I incurred; but the moment I saw the figures made all the hard work and expense totally worthwhile.

My aim then, as it remains today, was to help collectors get the figures they needed. By the time I factored in all my additional costs, each figure had now cost me around £8. I made the blisters available at a price of £15 each or £125 for a full set of ten and, needless to say, all my stock was sold within a 24-hour period. The sets I acquired are, to my knowledge, the only ones ever to have been imported.

Their value has certainly risen since then and they're now notoriously problematic to acquire. The price I put on a full set would now just about get you the Messi blister pack, with Cristiano Ronaldo also selling for around the £125 price mark.

As for the other eight figures in the set, their value rests at around £30-50 per blister, and I would estimate a full set of blisters would set you back around £600, my personal favourite from the set being Adriano in Inter Milan home kit.

Conventional Wisdom

The highlight of the Corinthian collecting calendar was always the Corinthian Convention, which would take place annually at Villa Park in April, May or June, depending on the ground's availability.

Corinthian held their first convention as part of a memorabilia show at the NEC in Birmingham in April 1999, however from 2000 through to 2007 they hosted their own dedicated Corinthian Convention, creating a Convention Special which was only made available to

purchase at the event. Unfortunately, due to unforeseen circumstances, the 2008 convention had to be cancelled.

My dad's family is from Cannock, which is not too far from Villa Park, so we would travel down and stay with my Gran on the Friday night. My uncles took me out for a few drinks, and it would be an understatement to say I was worse for wear on the morning of the convention; however, my Gran's fry-up and some fresh air in the queue waiting to go in soon sorted me out.

Corinthian produced some special products to be released at the convention, with special guests on hand to sign their blister packs, legends like Peter Shilton and Luther Blissett.

In addition to the special guests, Corinthian also had

a model maker's table where the figure sculptors were displaying their skills. While most collectors raced towards the array of figures on offer, I was having lengthy discussions with the sculptors, watching them sculpt a piece of modelling clay into a recognisable football star.

On the table were some models that I'd never seen before, and have certainly never seen since. Some, such as the Ronaldinho in England home kit, were auctioned

off, whereas I have no clue where the Aston Villa Fan Favourites Master Models ended up, nor the Frank Rijkaard manager sculpt.

I am fortunate to have in my personal collection a one-off sculpt of Ronaldo that was created at a convention by one of the sculptors. It's a version of Ronaldo that was never intended for release, having been sculpted in public as an example of the skills involved in the model-making process. A prize piece in my collection.

Then there was the official Corinthian shop with all the new releases and where, in true Corinthian form, you received free product for money spent: every £20 spent earned you a free Platinum pack, while a £50 spend got you one of the newly released Select 500 blister packs.

The free product was of course given out at random; but the Corinthian staff were very sympathetic and obliging, and I was able to request which figure I wanted. A bit of friendly banter and a smile go a long way.

One of the many highlights of the convention was the Pick 'n' Mix area, which was essentially large containers filled with figures. As the name suggests, it was a complete mix of product, everything from loose figures to blister packs. It really was immense fun, digging and delving to see what you could find, with Corinthian teasing that they had placed some really rare figures inside.

Even better than the picking and mixing, my personal favourite section was the trader tables, where it was possible to meet the sellers and collectors with whom you had communicated, and also a great place to forge valuable new contacts. The range of figures on offer from some of the traders was mind blowing, and for a young collector with some disposable income saved up, this was close to paradise.

There were also some large glass display cabinets which showcased figures being released. They often featured unreleased Master Models, along with an exclusive preview of products that were soon to be added to the production line.

Corinthian also held a live Master Model auction, where collectors fought fiercely to win, with large sums of money being paid, especially for those that were unreleased. I didn't get to attend these auctions, as I was just 20 when I attended my first convention in 2006, and the Master Models were then well beyond my financial reach.

Those collectors who attended the conventions all have fond memories. They really were superb events, and there's always been conversation between collectors about holding another one. So far, this is yet to happen, but who knows what the future holds?

Japan's New Wave of Corinthians

Corinthian collecting in Japan, and indeed the Far East in general, was truly at its peak during the early 2000s. That's when Corinthian's Japanese distributor, 'New Wave', ran the chain of sports stores called 'Foot Circle' and enjoyed an ever-increasing influence over the figures being produced as well as the volumes manufactured.

There were a few initial Japan-only release specials, and by 2002 there was a Japan Collector's Club, whose membership package included four exclusive figures: these were Javier Saviola in Barcelona away kit; Alessandro Del Piero in Juventus third kit; the excellent sculpt of David Beckham complete with Mohawk haircut in England long-sleeve shirt, and – last but certainly not least – the set was completed by Luis Figo in Real Madrid away kit.

I know what you're thinking: I said earlier that the Real Madrid deal collapsed, and indeed it did. So how come Luis Figo is in the Real Madrid kit? I can only speculate as

to why this Figo was allowed to be released; perhaps it was already too late to pull it, or perhaps Corinthian felt that as it was not being sold via any retail outlet, the normal licensing parameters did not apply.

Rumour has it that representatives of Real Madrid were aware of the Figo figure and contacted Corinthian for an explanation, requesting all stock to be destroyed; but this is just hearsay. In any case, Corinthian stated that the figure had been produced and released before the deal was cancelled, agreeing to destroy all remaining stock although a certain amount had already been distributed to collectors via the membership packs.

The Figo figure in the Real Madrid kit serves as a constant reminder to collectors of what we should have had, and is the only Real Madrid figure released by Corinthian. Value-wise, they go for roughly £15/20 each in a sealed sachet.

Corinthian also released a whole host of special figures exclusively for the Japanese market. The reason behind this exclusivity was largely down to image rights and Corinthian not being allowed to sell figures of players in J-League kits: that's why Corinthian could sell the Patrick Mboma figures in Cameroon kit but not ones in Vissel Kobe kits.

Patrick Mboma was also pencilled in for a release in Tokyo Verdy kit, before it was sadly cancelled – although the unreleased Master

Model does survive in my personal collection.

Possibly my favourite set from Japan are the eight Kashima Antlers blisters. All four figures are Brazilian – Bismarck, Jorginho, Alcindo and Leonardo – and come in home and away kits. The kit replication is right up there among Corinthian's finest work. You can expect to pay around £10-15 per blister, but although it's not an expensive series, acquiring all eight can prove difficult.

On the subject of kit replication, it would be remiss not to mention the exceptional kits Corinthian replicated on the Antônio Careca for Kashiwa Reysol and Ramón Díaz for Yokohama Marinos. It's worth taking the effort to acquire all four figures, which are of similar value to the Kashima Antlers, around £15 each.

Lucky Boxes and Bags - Or Were They?

During the early-2000s peak of Corinthian collecting in Japan, products and series were being designed exclusively for this lucrative market. The Japanese customer has always liked the idea of a mystery box, with the Corinthian Miniatures range all being sold in that format, so at the Japanese distributors' request, Corinthian produced the 'Lucky Box'

This was a cardboard box that contained a single ProStars blister pack or window box from all figures released so far, a ProStars sealed sachet, and a MicroStars figure – there being a one-in-50 chance of landing one of the four exclusive Lucky Box blister packs.

The product was sold in Japan in 2003 but Corinthian did obtain limited stock which it made available to UK customers from the autumn of that year, with the Lucky Box being priced at £7.

The four figures you were hoping to find inside were Rivaldo in Brazil away kit, Javier Saviola in Barcelona home kit, Ruud Van Nistelrooy in Holland away kit and Sergio Conceicao in Inter Milan home kit; you will notice it is the exact same set of four figures that were released as Memorabilia specials. This is actually the only blister pack version of Saviola ever released, all other releases were as a clear sachet.

It was never disclosed how many of each were actually produced but they have always remained elusive, so I do think it was relatively low. It has always appeared to me that the Conceicao is the rarest, followed by Saviola, with Rivaldo and Van Nistelrooy certainly seeming to come to

market more frequently.

This is quite a rare set and certainly worth picking up, should you get the chance. Conceicao could set you back around £50, with Saviola not too far behind, while Rivaldo and Van Nistelrooy can be bought for around £30.

Corinthians' Japanese distributor 'New Wave' requested four exclusive figures to be used in their Lucky Bag launched on 1st January 2006, with each bag containing approximately 25 figures from previously released stock, along with two of the new, exclusive figures, packed at random.

The Lucky Bag cost ¥10,000, which back in 2006 was roughly £50, and although it was just a stock-clearing exercise, you at least had the guarantee of getting two exclusive figures in each bag – unlike the previous so called 'Lucky Boxes' where the promise of an exclusive blister or Select 500 never materialised.

The four figures selected are Adriano in Parma home kit from the 2002/03 season, Robbie Fowler in 2005/06 Manchester City away kit, Manuel Rui Costa in AC Milan 2005/06 away kit and Damiano Tommasi in Italy 2005/06 home kit.

Corinthian only manufactured 800 of each figure, and it has always been the Tommasi that has been harder to find, a fact that I've always attributed to Italian kit figures being so popular in Japan.

Pricewise, Fowler and Rui Costa can be picked up for around £10 and Adriano is more in the £15-20 region, while a Tommasi could set you back roughly £30.

Vialli Heads to Smith's

This figure is one of the rarest Corinthian released as part of the ProStars range, as it had a very unusual method of release.

The figure of Gianluca Vialli in Chelsea away kit was only available by purchasing a Chelsea VHS tape from participating WHSmith stores in the UK. The VHS tape was the *Chelsea Official Review of the 1998/99 Season*, which had Vialli on the front cover, as he was the club's player-manager at that time.

The promotion didn't run for a prolonged period of time, and while a giveaway figure might seem, at first glance, unlikely to end up on the rare list, there were several other factors which contributed to the figure becoming hard to find.

Firstly, although the stocks were sent to stores, it was then reliant on the store staff to ensure that the figure was correctly given away when the video purchase was made. In reality, it's apparent that very few of the figures ever made it into circulation. The Vialli figure was not packaged inside or attached to the VHS box, you needed to request it at the till, and given how precious few Viallis are around now, it's safe to assume many purchasers of the tape missed out.

Another reason perhaps veers more into the territory of myth; but it was always rumoured that unused stock of the Vialli was sent back to Corinthian to be destroyed.

I am never one to accept such stories without proof, but given the fact that you'll perhaps see one Vialli a year for sale, the speculation does appear to be plausible. If the stock were not destroyed, then the figures would have ended up in the hands of collectors by other means, and it's clear that is not the case. It has also been suggested that keen Corinthian employees ventured into a skip in an attempt to retrieve the Vialli figures; but, apparently with little to show for their alleged efforts.

A loose Vialli can command £75, and if you're fortunate to be offered a sealed sachet then I feel you could be expected to pay in the region of £125-150. Why not go one step further, like I did, and actually purchase the Chelsea season review VHS tape?

What many collectors may not know is that the initial plan was for the Vialli to actually be in the long-sleeve away kit; but this would have required a new manufacturing tool, which would have dramatically increased both the cost and production time. As a result, the idea was changed to simply use the existing Vialli figure. Only the unreleased long-sleeve Master Model exists.

Corinthians Eclipse the Competition

Corinthian teamed up with confectionary giant McVitie's to produce a special set of four Manchester United figures, which were given away with promotional packs of Jaffa Cakes.

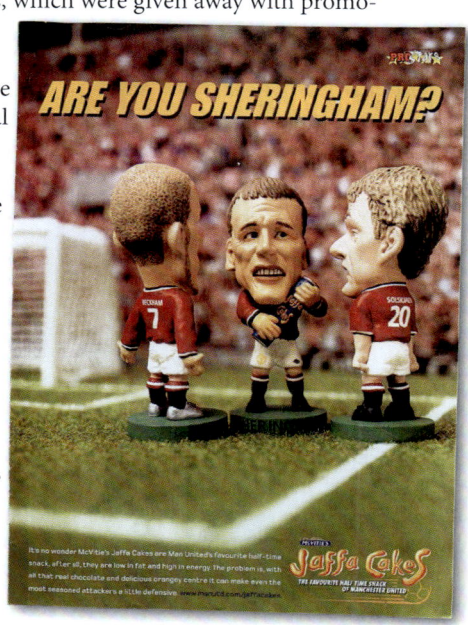

Whether you were a half moon or total eclipse, everyone loved Jaffa Cakes, so when there were also Corinthian figures on offer – well, that made them pretty much irresistible.

The four figures in Manchester United home kit are Fabien Barthez, Ryan Giggs, Paul Scholes and David Beckham, each coming in a sealed clear sachet with a collector card. Of course, the figures were presented on a vibrant orange base, each assigned a collector code beginning with JC.

As cool as the figures are, what really caught collectors' attention, and has been discussed for over 20 years, are the figures shown in the advertisement posters that appeared in *Match* magazine. Corinthian produced three outstanding posters to promote the range, all with excellent slogans and featuring truly eye-catching figures.

'Deadly, Once They're in the Box' shows Ryan Giggs holding a box of Jaffa Cakes, with David Beckham and Paul Scholes reaching to grab one.

'Are you Sheringham?' has Teddy Sheringham clutching a tube of Jaffa Cakes with Beckham and Solskjaer annoyed and angry at his reluctance to share.

'They're Just Impossible to Save' has Fabien Barthez with chocolate around his lips, with Jaap Stam and Gary Neville looking displeased that all the Jaffa Cakes are gone.

It truly is a tragedy that Corinthian didn't release these

exceptional figures. Unfortunately, only the Master Models exist. So, what happened to them? Well, the Paul Scholes appeared for sale on Japanese website Madbooth, and it has always been my assumption that the other models suffered the same fate and were simply sold to Japan, never to be seen again.

Lucozade Figures with Collector Cards?

Corinthian were doing numerous cross-brand promotions at this point, all in an effort to increase brand awareness and get their product into as many countries as possible, and there was no bigger emerging market than China.

Corinthian teamed up with soft drinks company Lucozade to release a set of eight figures in China, to be given away with bottles of Lucozade Sport. The figures had all previously been released by Corinthian, with each one sold in a special Lucozade-branded window box. There are four Liverpool and four Manchester United figures.

The former came from the Liverpool 2000/01 Treble Winners set, with Stéphane Henchoz, Steven Gerrard and Robbie Fowler appearing in home kit and Michael Owen in away kit.

As for Manchester United, the quartet were Fabien Barthez who was in ProStars Series 9, Roy Keane who is the ProStars Series 10 figure, Andy Cole who was in ProStars Series 12 and Ryan Giggs who was part of the Collector's Edition Series.

The figures were released in sets of two, and were available for two weeks before a new set was introduced. The sets and release dates were detailed on the window box and were as follows:

```
07/11/01 - 20/11/01 = Roy Keane & Robbie Fowler
21/11/01 - 04/12/01 = Andy Cole & Michael Owen
05/12/01 - 18/12/01 = Fabien Barthez & Stéphane Henchoz
19/12/01 - 01/01/02 = Ryan Giggs & Steven Gerrard
```

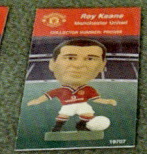

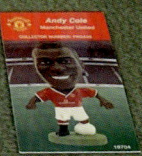

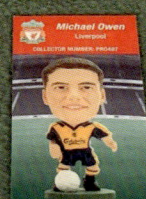
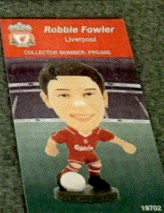

Of course, the figures themselves are very common due to them not being exclusive and featuring in other ProStars series; but these Lucozade Sport window boxes are incredibly rare and are seldom seen for sale, so a full set of eight could set you back £150.

During the process of writing this book I reacquired a set of these Lucozade window boxes, having sold numerous other sets over the years. The Henchoz figure was off-centre so, wanting to adjust it, I opened the box to remove the figure tray and a collector card fell out and hit the floor – as did my jaw.

Picking the card up, I instantly realised it was a different version to the one included in the Liverpool Treble Winners Cup Team Pack, with the figure image on the generic ProStars series background.

I checked all eight window boxes and, to my amazement, each one had a variant collector card. Given the complexity involved with obtaining these cards and how seldom you actually see the window boxes for sale, they have to be right up there with the rarest collector cards in the ProStars range. The complete set in my collection is the only full set I've ever seen.

Do you have the energy to find all eight exclusive Lucozade collector cards?

Collector Card Variants and Errors

It wasn't just the Corinthian figures that came with variants and errors but the collector cards, too. As collectors, we don't mind the odd typo or misspelt name, as it gives us something extra to collect.

The first error appeared in ProStars Series 3 England Legends, when Corinthian mixed up the figure images on the Nat Lofthouse and Tom Finney cards, and on the Robbie Fowler PRO098 and PRO156 cards the reverse of his card has the player's surname spelt as 'Flower'.

The Platinum blister pack of Frank Lampard in ProStars Series 13 has Chelsea incorrectly spelt as 'Cheslea'; but what's really odd is that the card error solely appears in the Platinum pack. Another spelling mistake appears in ProStars Series 31, the PRO1362 figure of Shunsuke Nakamura has his first name misspelt as 'Shinsuke'.

Jari Litmanen PRO466 appears in ProStars Series 13 and was also included in the UK version of the Liverpool Treble Cup Winners Team Pack, with each version having its own collector card.

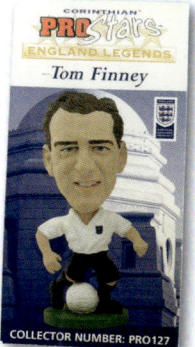

Celtic requested some figures to be repacked into a custom green-and-white blister pack to be sold specifically in the club shop, and from these five blisters we also get variant collector cards. The figures are Martin O'Neill PRO368, Henrik Larsson PRO461, Neil Lennon PRO510 and PRO540, with of course the Nakamura PRO1362 also having a variant card. The Larsson and Lennon home kit variant cards are only something that I discovered in the last year.

ProStars Series 21 saw Corinthian make another improvement to their product: each blister pack now came with an individually numbered collector card, which stated how many were produced, making every blister unique and further enhancing their collectable aspect.

Corinthian also made the figures available direct from themselves in 'clear sachet with collector card' format, priced at £2.49. As these collector cards were not part of the blister-pack production volume, the cards were not individually numbered and instead have the figure images on both sides of the card.

The 16 regular release figures in Series 21 and 22 all have those variant collector cards, making it another 32 for the collection – and finding them all is no easy task.

We also have a variant collector card in the Club Gold World Greats range as Set J contains Fredrik Ljungberg for Sweden; however, there was some confusion over the kit he was going to be released in, with the initial application poster depicting the player in a white and yellow away kit, rather than the dark blue kit he would eventually appear wearing.

The collector card that accompanied the figure was actually the unreleased white and yellow kit version, and it wasn't until the summer of 2020 that it was realised that in fact both versions of the collector card exist.

PRO211 - Do You Owen All Four?

Michael Owen was rapidly establishing himself as an elite striker in world football, following an impressive performance in the 1998 World Cup in France. Corinthian knew demand for his first figure would be high, so they went ahead and produced him in four different body poses as part of ProStars Series 2 Secret Sachet; there was even a 'Michael Owen inside this pack' sticker on his particular sachet, the collector codes being PRO050, 51, 52 and 53.

Corinthian would release a Liverpool 12-figure team pack for the 1999/2000 season with Owen included, his

collector code being PRO211. However, in appearance the figure is identical to that released in Series 2 Secret Sachet. Of course, to many this will be information you already know; but were you aware of the further complication to the story? Three different body poses of Owen are actually found in the pack, all with collector code PRO211...

The one most commonly found is the one as shown on the collector card, which is pose 3, however pose 1 and pose 2 were also made with PRO211. The pose 1 version does appear every now and then, but pose 2 is notoriously difficult to find. This is not the end of the revelations, though: Corinthian also released pose 4 as PRO211, this version exclusively inside the Platinum pack which came issued with the team pack.

I've collected all the 1999/2000 club team-pack Platinums and I can say from my personal experience that Liverpool were by far the hardest to complete, in fact Owen was the penultimate Platinum I needed.

To the best of my knowledge, Corinthian never disclosed this information to collectors, and I'm quite confident they weren't even aware of it themselves. It is possible that the factory did this under their own volition.

A possible theory is that the factory didn't have enough Owen figures of pose 3 to complete the production run, so simply used the other poses to finish off the job.

I myself discovered this and became consciously aware of the existence of all four in 2023 when I purchased a Liverpool 1999/2000 team pack off eBay, and when it arrived the Owen was pose 1 but with collector code PRO211.

I feel, after reading this, there might be an influx of collectors scouring eBay in the hope of finding all versions of Michael Owen PRO211. Do you Ow(e)n all four?

Club Gold World Greats

Corinthian launched the ProStars Club Gold World Greats range as part of the 2000 Collector Club package and offered some exclusive products to those who joined, tempting us with three different levels of membership: Silver, Gold and Platinum.

Perhaps the most iconic football player ever is the legendary Pelé, with Corinthian releasing him as part of Set A. My brother and I combined our pocket money to join the Corinthian Collector Club at Silver level to ensure we got the Pelé figure. Its value has fluctuated over the years, though I believe a current guide price would be around £75. Alfredo Di Stéfano in Argentina home kit from Set C is one of the most valuable examples from the entire Club Gold World Greats collection, which I have seen sell for in excess of £100.

One of my personal favourites comes from Set D, with the world's most recognisable referee Pierluigi Collina released, eyes wide and brandishing a red card. My brother and I then had to rejoin the Collector Club purely to secure this figure. It was money well spent.

Set H contains the excellent figure of Colombian Carlos Valderrama, a figure whose price did drop a little when Corinthian released his figure again as part of the ProStars Classics range, but this original release can still fetch in the region of £40.

Set I is, for me, the most expensive and troublesome set to complete, as it features Zico, Paolo Rossi and Jean Tigana. Value-wise, Zico can command over £100, Rossi £75 and Tigana £50 but all three are notoriously difficult to find.

The Corinthian Collector Club later received a makeover and a restructuring, doing away with the three established levels of membership and adopting instead a two-tier system, SuperStars and Legends.

And so, on 1st March 2005, the ProStars Collector Club 2005 was launched. The SuperStars membership cost just £10 and came with four exclusive figures, the premium option much more pricy at £55, but coming with 12 exclusive figures which were all first-time sculpts, only one of them ever being reused by Corinthian.

This 2005 set features the excellent Eusebio; incredible to think this was the only regular ProStars figure made of him by Corinthian, selling for about £30. The undoubted highlight of this set is René Higuita, the eccentric keeper best known for his audacious scorpion kick to clear the ball off the line against England at Wembley in 1995, his figure selling for around £75.

The 2006 Legends membership contained a truly star-studded line-up and some eternally in-demand figures, such as Preben Elkjaer, Ruud Krol, Leopold Luque, Rudi Voller and Spain goalkeeper Andoni Zubizarreta. You must expect to pay around £40 for any of those.

Corinthian released an exceptional new sculpt of Eric Cantona in France home kit, and adding 'King Eric' to your collection can set you back over £60. But all these figures are totally eclipsed by the most sought after and valuable figure in the entire Club Gold range, Lev Yashin.

This is the only figure Corinthian released of the legendary Russian shotstopper. Even loose you can expect to part with a minimum of £75, and getting one in a window box is going to cost around twice that much, though it's probably only one per year that appears for sale.

2007 was the final year of the Corinthian Collector Club, and they bowed out in style with eight excellent figures. Luigi Riva may be a relative unknown to some younger collectors, but those of a certain vintage will remember the Italian striker. His figure sells for around £40, likewise the excellent fresh sculpt of Swede Henrik Larsson.

The rarest figure from this set is without question that of Paul Breitner in West Germany home kit, seldom seen for sale, but when he does appear the price tag is around £50.

Corinthians Return to Woolworths

2005 saw Corinthian ProStars figures make a return to major retail stores, with Corinthian launching the ProStars Retail Series. The figures were sold in stores such as Woolworths, Toymaster, Toys 'R' Us, Hamleys and The Entertainer, as well as being available from Corinthian Direct.

Personally speaking, it was amazing to see Corinthian figures back in a retail store. By this point there were some excellent and well-established online retailers but you simply couldn't beat flicking the racks and picking off a blister pack with your own hands.

The highlight of the initial release was the double packs. I can still recall picking up the Manchester United and Everton packs from Woolies, as the United pack had O'Shea's first release while the Toffees' two pack contained McFadden.

In true Corinthian form, a series was released to coincide with the 2006 World Cup, but for the seasoned collector it offered little to inspire, the exception being the England figures in away kit. It's worth mentioning that the quiz card that came with the Rooney away kit figure has the home kit figure image on it, another little Corinthian mistake.

I remember the home kit figures being sold off at 50p once England were knocked out of the tournament at the quarter-final stage on penalties to Portugal.

My personal highlight from the entire ProStars Retail range is the redemption figure of Robinho in Brazil home kit. You needed just four tokens to claim one of the four redemption figures, the other three being Adriano, Pablo Aimar and Andriy Shevchenko.

It truly was awesome to once again see and be able to buy Corinthian ProStars in a physical store, but from a collector's standpoint the range never really captured the imagination, and I suspect by this time there was a dedicated collector fanbase who remained loyal to the online retailers.

Fan Favourites vs Collector Favourites

Corinthian released a new style of ProStars figure in the latter part of 2003, called ProStars Fan Favourites. The figures are the same size as ProStars, they carry their own collector code, which starts with FF, but they are a two-piece mould, meaning their heads are a separate piece to the body, which also allows them to turn.

Predominantly a team-pack product, the general consensus is that collectors loved the idea of a single pack containing a full starting 11, which saw six players stood up and six crouched down, with the captain having the ball at his feet – although there was a downside in that the two-piece mould lent the figures a cheaper look and feel.

The two most sought-after team packs are Manchester United 1968 and the Middlesbrough League Cup Winners Celebration pack. The United pack is often required by collectors as it contains Sir Matt Busby, so it maintains a value of around £100. As for the Boro pack, it's seldom seen for sale but when it does become available you can expect to pay £125-£150.

Something that perplexed collectors at this time was the reason why neither of these team packs came complete with collector cards – and the reason would seem to be an administrative one. From what I've been told from multiple reliable sources, Corinthian simply neglected to tick the box for collector cards when submitting the final production sheet to the manufacturer.

It may also come as a surprise to know that Corinthian also planned to release a Juventus Fan Favourites team pack as well as one for Rangers. I've seen 14 different sculpts

done for Juventus: Gianluigi Buffon, Alessandro Del Piero, Alessandro Tacchinardi, David Trezeguet, Edgar Davids, Fabrizio Miccoli, Gianluca Zambrotta, Pavel Nedvěd, Igor Tudor, Lilian Thuram, Marco Di Vaio, Mark Iluiano, Marco Camoranesi and Paolo Montero.

As for Rangers, I believe there were 17 different Master Models sculpted: Stefan Klos, Michael Ball, Barry Ferguson, Claudio Caniggia, Christian Nerlinger, Craig Moore, Fernando Ricksen, Kevin Muscat, Maurice Ross, Michael Mols, Mikel Arteta, Neil McCann, Nuno Capucho, Peter Lovenkrands, Lorenzo Amoruso, Ronald de Boer and Shota Averladze.

I'm proud to say that 16 of those unreleased Rangers Master Models are in my personal collection. The only one that still evades me is the Lorenzo Amoruso – hopefully one day I can complete the set.

Peru's Second-best Export

Of course, Peru's most celebrated export is Paddington Bear, but in the world of Corinthian there's another product that runs him a close second: the ProStars Fan Favourites two-pack blisters. I know many reading this will wonder what I'm blathering on about. Well, why don't you grab a marmalade sandwich and let me explain?

Corinthian were asked by a department store based in Peru called *Saga Falabella* to produce a range of 36 ProStars Fan Favourites figures, the set mooted to cover current stars as well as legends and icons of the game.

From 1st March 2005, collectors could order the full set

of 36 figures in clear sachet format from Corinthian direct at a cost of £100, and they were also given away as a free gift when purchases were made over a certain order value.

The set was also released in Japan but as a 'blind box' product, which had the figures still in clear sachet with collector card and a collector's information leaflet, but placed inside packaging with no clue as to what was inside. Each CDU (counter display unit) held 15 blind boxes. There were 48 different figures in the Japan blind box release, the 36 Peru *Saga Falabella* figures and 12 others from the club team packs.

The figures were initially sold in a two-pack blister, with each containing the two figures and collector cards. So there were 18 different two-pack blisters produced in all, which were sold exclusively in *Saga Falabella* stores in Peru. I've personally only ever seen two different blisters: the two pack of Kaká and Shevchenko for AC Milan is from my own personal collection, and I've once laid eyes on the Maradona and Careca blister; the other 16 packs I've never seen, but can only assume they do exist.

These two-pack blisters have to be considered as among the rarest, if not the rarest set of blisters ever released by Corinthian in the ProStars range. I've tried in vain to locate additional packs but have never even come close. I wonder if I might need to enlist the help of that famous bear?

Corinthian Gets Bigger and Better

Corinthian experienced success with the XL range of Headliners, the figures being more fragile and 15cm in height – so it was no great surprise to see them next release some XL ProStars, starting off with the Millennium series, which brought together ten legends of the game.

Those ten legends are Pelé, Ferenc Puskás, Bobby Moore, Gordon Banks, Michel Platini, Diego Maradona, George Best, Johan Cruyff, Franz Beckenbauer and Eusebio, and a full set can set you back £250 – a far cry from when they were being sold off in Poundstretcher for £2!

The XL figures of Carlos Tevez and Cristiano Ronaldo

are amongst the rarest in the series, very seldom do you see them for sale. Tevez can easily command £50 and CR7 can set you back over £75.

There are 52 different XL ProStars but the collector codes stop at XL053 – so which one is missing? That's XL047, which was supposed to be Zinedine Zidane in Juventus away kit, however this figure was sadly cancelled, with the Master Model being sold off by Corinthian.

My personal favourite release is the Roberto Baggio two pack which features him in the Italy national home and away kits, as worn at the USA 1994 World Cup. I'm unsure as to how many two packs were made as the certificates are numbered but they're the same ones as used in the single boxes; a further note is that the certificates in the two pack are not identical for the home and away kit as you might imagine, the numbers are different and not sequential.

I'm often asked why there are precious few XL Master Models around. The reason is that when Corinthian was moving offices, the vast majority were dropped and broken during transit! I am pleased to say I have three unreleased XL Master Models in my collection: the tooling master of Roberto Di Matteo, along with painted masters of Andy Cole for Manchester United and a simply superb manager sculpt of Ruud Gullit.

It's Official

In the entire Corinthian collection, the figures of team and football officials – managers, coaches and referees – are amongst the most popular, with many collectors choosing to collect all those that were released.

As part of the Headliners range there are 13 managers and one coach, Brian Kidd for Manchester United. This figure is unique in that it's the only one released in that particular body pose, holding a clipboard.

The majority of these managers are quite accessible, the exception being Souness for Southampton who can set you back around £40.

There are 32 managers in the regular ProStars range, along with referees Dermot Gallagher and Pierlugi Collina. My personal highlights would have to include the excellent sculpt of Brian Clough, complete with his iconic green sweatshirt.

Two legendary England managers, Sir Alf Ramsey and Sir Bobby Robson, got their solitary release, and I must mention David Moyes, who was released in a unique body pose wearing a tracksuit. No other figure was released in this particular pose.

As part of the Club Gold range there are nine managers plus referee Pierluigi Collina, a truly exceptional sculpt and a figure which has always been highly revered by collectors.

We have three in the ProStars Retail range and just two as part of the Fan Favourites range, though they are its two rarest figures: Sir Matt Busby for Manchester United and Steve McClaren for Middlesbrough. Completing the collection of managers is Sir Alex Ferguson from the Pepsi release.

So, it's official...

In total, there are 64 managers, coaches and referees to collect as part of the Headliners and ProStars collection.

MICROSTARS 2001-2011

"Football Crazy, Chocolate Mad...

"**G**rab a Powerpodz and play football with the lads!" I certainly hope you remember singing that jingle, it truly is an iconic advert and even those who wouldn't call themselves Corinthian collectors recall it fondly. On 12th February 2001, after over two years of product development, MicroStars were born!

Corinthian had reached an exclusive agreement with the UK's biggest producer of Easter eggs, Magna Confectionery Ltd, to pack and release the MicroStars figures inside hollow chocolate shells, called Powerpodz! The figures were packed into a clear sachet and then placed into a plastic capsule, along with a collector's information leaflet.

The cost of packing the figures inside a hollow chocolate shell was only marginally more than releasing it in a clear sachet or window box, and less than the cost of a blister pack. Perhaps the biggest advantage of the Powerpodz was that they were able to be sold in a much broader range of high-street stores, from major retailers like Woolworths, Asda and Sainsbury's to a whole host of newsagents and garages, meaning MicroStars were literally everywhere.

163

The main difference that MicroStars have over Headliners/ProStars is that under the base was some player skill ratings. MicroStars were predominantly aimed at a younger demographic, with a price point of just £1.49, so a game was devised, which started out as a 'One on One' and evolved later into the World Club League.

The five base ratings were Dribbling, Shooting, Tackling, Passing and Crossing, with the goalkeepers having two ratings, Save Shot Left and Save Shot Right. The figures were initially released on six different base colours – green, red, blue, white, silver and gold – the base ratings increasing along with the rarity of the base. Anyone who ever purchased a PowerPodz can still recall the taste of the chocolate used. I'm fortunate to have a still-intact MicroStars Powerpodz in my collection, although I'm certainly not going to eat it. It's far too collectible for that – and would also be far too injurious to my health!

Last-minute Moves and Rug Rethinks

Right at the start of MicroStars' life there was controversy and mystique around the figures, all caused by a haircut and a club transfer.

Henrik Larsson was a huge star for Celtic, and his dreadlocks were almost as famous in their own right. It shocked the football world when the Swedish striker shaved off his locks, and it also created a problem for Corinthian.

A dreadlocked version of Henrik Larsson for Celtic was

planned for inclusion in the first range of PowerPodz, however he chopped off his hairstyle just as Corinthian had begun production, so this version was cancelled and we would have to wait until Series 3 for his release, where we got a shaven-headed version of the super Swede.

The dreadlocked version of Larsson may have been cancelled but Corinthian had already produced a few pre-

We were going to start the Celtic collection with Henrik Larsson.

As we started production he cut his famous dreadlocks off, so we decided to withdraw him from the range.

A shaven headed Larsson will be available later in the year.

LARSSON
UNRELEASED MODEL

production samples. These are the regular figures but have a more hollow base without the player stats. There can only be a handful of these in existence and they're highly sought after by collectors – you can effectively name your price if you have an example to sell.

We come to the infamous Tore Andre Flo in Chelsea home kit. Flo transferred to Rangers from Chelsea just after Corinthian had finished production. Efforts were made in the factory to remove him from the shipment but, according to Corinthian, 4,600 had already been packed and distributed to shops.

Tore Andre Flo transferred to Rangers just as our production had finished.

We were able to stop his inclusion as a Chelsea player, but 4,600 pieces had already been packed.

This Flo model is sure to become one of the first MicroStars collectors items. Keep hold of him if you find one!

FLO

I've always been extremely sceptical about that number but given the sheer volume of PowerPodz produced it is also plausible that it's accurate. Most collectors consider this Chelsea version of Flo an unreleased figure, and it is regarded by many as a 'Holy Grail' piece.

Over the years, I've seen very few Flos appear for sale; you'd think if 4,600 were made then it would be more prevalent, but that is simply not the case. Corinthian themselves did auction off a couple of these Chelsea Flos, and I've also seen a couple in sealed sachet trade hands amongst collectors. As with the Larsson, you can name your price if you want to sell a Chelsea Flo: many desire the figure for their collection but very few are prepared to pay the huge transfer fee it would command.

Thanks again to Lennart Van de Winkel for allowing me to use the images of Henrik Larrson with dreadlocks and Tore Andre Flo Chelsea kit from his personal collection.

Take a Look Behind the Camera

Here, I'll try to explain the myth and legend that surrounds perhaps the rarest MicroStars figure ever, which – rather obscurely, and in true Corinthian form – is not a player but a TV camera!

Corinthian released four series of MicroStars in Mexico, which were done in association with Deportes, a local broadcasting company. Mexico Series 1 saw four Deportes Reporters released: Javier Alarcón González, Raúl Orvañanos Marin, Enrique Bermúdez de la Serna 'Perro' and Antonio de Valdés Franco 'Tono', with all four being released solely on a green base.

Mexico Series 2 saw a further four Deportes Reporters released: Ricardo Peláez, Alberto García Aspe, Miguel Gurwitz and Raúl Sarmiento, again all four being released only on a green base. The same quartet were then released again as part of Mexico Series 4. With Aspe by far the rarest of all the eight Deportes Reporters, completing the set is no easy task.

So we come to the now legendary and infamous MC3876 Deportes Televisa Camera. Over the years, there have been numerous rumours as to how this figure may have been released. Some claim it was sent along with the Mexico Series store display, taped to the underside of the box and possibly thrown away without stockists realising.

Others have claimed they were visible on store counters as promotional pieces, and a few deny its existence altogether.

There's no mention of the Televisa Camera anywhere on Mexico Series 1 box, CDU or collector's information leaflet. I feel had this been some sort of chaser figure for the series and issued for general release, then there would have been some mention of it, to drive sales, as any marketing team would surely have flagged up the lure of chasing a rare and exclusive item.

So, my personal feeling is that the Camera was never part of a released series, and never available for direct sale – and, for that reason, I don't think it can be included as part of the released collection. My feeling has remained the same all these years, which is that a very small number of the Televisa Cameras were produced for marketing purposes, and some may very well have been on display in stores to promote the range. Whatever the case, I doubt we'll ever know now with utter certainty; but nevertheless the camera does remain an incredibly rare MicroStars figure, and one which is coveted by each and every MicroStars collector.

Muchas gracias to Victor Gonzalez for assistance with the information, and to Lennart Van de Winkel for providing the pictures of the superb TV Camera from his personal collection. I would also like to pay my respects here to Victor Hugo Rivera Arellano, a fierce and passionate collector who passed away a few years back.

Fanaticos Drive Collectors to Drink…

The Corinthian Coca-Cola Mundialistas box set saw the inclusion of six Fanaticos figures, which were fan-style figures, however Corinthian also released a further two Fanatico figures.

The other two Fanaticos are of Brazil and Germany fans, and they were released in McDonald's in South America, most notably in Venezuela and El Salvador. They were released in a secret sachet given away when purchasing the South American version of a McDonald's Happy Meal, the name given to these sachets being *Los Microhinchas*

Mundialistas De Coca-Cola, which translates to English as 'World Cup Micro Fans of Coca-Cola'

Their existence was never truly acknowledged by Corinthian; there's no mention of them in any of the Collector Club newsletters, and for a long time it was assumed by collectors that they were just two of the many MC code gaps in the MicroStars collection.

Adding the Brazil and Germany Fanatico figures to your collection is not as problematic as it used to be. They're by no means commonplace but they do appear with more regularity than they used to, with a price of around £75 each the usual going rate.

The sachet itself is also somewhat of a collector's item, and was something I wasn't even aware of until 2021. It was never listed nor mentioned by Corinthian in any of their newsletters. Again, the company had provided the kind of delayed-action bombshell that we all love them for.

Corinthian also sculpted a French and English Fanatico, with the French fan sculpted with goatee beard and holding an air horn.

Luca, the Updated Toni

Italy Series 4 would prove to be the final series that Corinthian would release in partnership with Giochi Preziosi, however Giochi would release two more series on their own, using the MicroStars branding as they acquired the name rights once Corinthian had ceased trading.

Italy Series 4 was released in February 2011, so was well into production by the time Luca Toni moved from Genoa to Juventus during the January transfer window.

It was much too late to pull the Genoa figure from the range, however inside each Toni in Genoa kit was a card which advertised the Juventus version. You needed to contact Giocho Preziosi and ask to be sent the Toni in Juventus kit as a free gift, with distribution being limited to one per household.

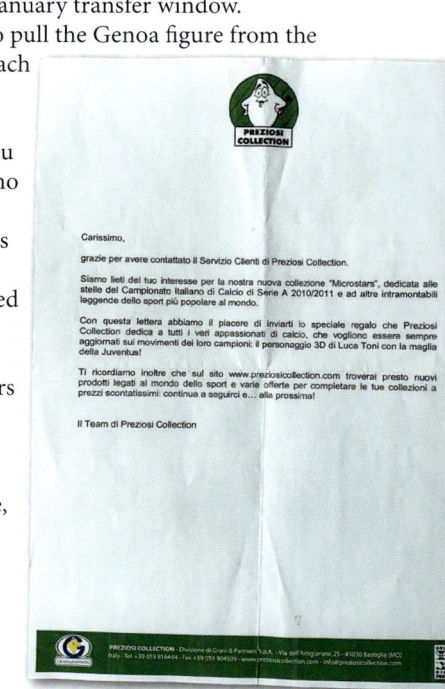

The Tonis in Juventus kit were sent to collectors in a clear sachet, also coming with a Juventus Fanbuk. He was only released on a green base, with the same MC code as the Genoa version, MC13180.

It is believed that just 1,500 Luca Toni in Juventus kit were made, and it took only a few months to exhaust all the stock. Soon these rare figures would appear on the secondary market for exorbitant prices. Especially when you consider that the figure was originally acquired for free, the sums Italian collectors were charging for the Toni were met with overwhelming disapproval from the collectors' community.

This has not changed in over a decade; the Toni is as rare as ever and I would expect you would need to part with in excess of £100 to acquire one... but it is an essential part of the collection.

Corinthian Make a Meal of It

2003 saw fast-food giant McDonald's team up with Corinthian to produce a set of football figures to be given away free with their iconic Happy Meal.

The figures were part of the MicroStars range, being assigned collector codes starting with MSE (MicroStars Special Edition) and being of a similar size to the regular MicroStars, however the figures were in sliding poses and on a oval base, which was much larger than the standard MicroStars base.

As with the regular MicroStars, these were also given player ratings, located under the base, the five ratings for outfield players being Cross, Pass, Dribble, Tackle and Shoot, while the goalkeepers were rated on 'Save shot to left' and 'right' – so these figures could also be used as part of the MicroStars WCL game.

The three countries taking part in this promotion were England, Scotland and Wales, each having its own version of the promotional Happy Meal: in England you could only get the England players, and so on. This is a major factor why the Scotland and, especially, the Wales figures are much harder to find than their English counterparts, as there were obviously a lot more participating McDonald's restaurants to be found in England than in Wales.

There were 11 England players to collect, with one being given away inside each McDonald's Happy Meal, the figures presented inside a plastic tray and placed inside a sealed white plastic bag. The Happy Meal box featured the 11 England players to collect, with a leaflet also coming issued with each Happy Meal.

The versions found in Scotland and Wales also had their

very own specific Happy Meal box design, coming with their own leaflet, too. As for the figures, the Scotland ones were in sealed blue plastic bags and the Welsh ones in red.

Dave Rule and Richard Balfre fondly recall making trips to McDonald's restaurants in both Wales and Scotland to acquire bundles of these figures to appease the collectors' market in Japan.

There was also a Micro Dome released as part of this promotion, with McDonald's logo and branding appearing on the front of dome, the decal stickers and hoardings. The full set of 20 figures also came in a specially designed plastic tray which houses them perfectly.

McDonald's employees could enter an MDUK Footie Special competition, with the Micro Dome being offered as a runners-up prize.

This really is an incredibly rare item; to the best of my knowledge, Corinthian made no mention of it in any of their newsletters, making it a real collector's piece.

MicroStars Fill the Stadium

Since the launch of MicroStars, Corinthian were inundated with requests to produce a display case or other product to accompany the figures, and on 18th October 2004 collectors' prayers were answered with the release of the Corinthian MicroStars Display Stands.

Corinthian produced two different stands, 'straight' and 'curved', the idea being to create a full MicroStars Stadium. The straight stands held 60 figures and the curved 50, with each tier having a thin slit which allowed the MicroStars figure to be slid in and held firmly in place.

To create a full MicroStars stadium, collectors needed to purchase six straight stands and four curved, in which case the capacity of your full three-dimensional MicroStars stadium would be 560 figures. Each Display Stand cost £5.99, so creating a full stadium would cost £60. Corinthian also included some stickers to be added to the stadium to give it an authentic look.

The MicroStars stands were, as you would imagine, incredibly popular, and are still highly sought after today, with boxed versions being notoriously difficult to pick up.

Collectors may not be aware that Corinthian also released a display stand as part of the German series, distributed by Simba. The name given to this product was Champions Gallery. The MicroStars Champions Gallery is a black, curved stand, which had the same figure slot system as the UK version, with space for 50 figures. It was sold exclusively in Germany.

Corinthian also released a display product as part of its

partnership with Giochi Preziosi, who were their Italian distributor. The MicroStars Bacheca was effectively a display case, it came with stickers and player-name stickers for all 40 figures in Italy Series 1. But there was a snag. The Bacheca only had space for 20 figures, so if you wanted to display the full series you would need to buy two.

It's an interesting, unique item that is certainly worth adding to the collection. A great way to display a small collection, but certainly not practical for displaying a larger one. This product was sold and distributed exclusively in Italy by Giochi Preziosi.

Thanks to Lennart Van de Winkel for providing the images of his impressive MicroStars Stadium.

Different Poses, and Colours to Boot

Although there aren't as many variants as in the Headliners and ProStars ranges, MicroStars does also have some of its own to find.

UK Series 13 sees Thierry Henry in France home (MC5420) and away kit (MC5739) in two different body poses: fists and fingers! The reason for this variant is that the factory ran out of Henry during production, so to meet the required amount they were forced to use the other pose they had available for him. The MC codes are identical for both versions, the alternate pose with the left arm horizontal to the body being the harder version to locate.

UK Series 14 presents our next variant, which is Michael Owen in Newcastle United home kit MC7729. The figure was released with two different boot colours, the more common version being that which matches the image provided by Corinthian, wearing white boots with a black trim. Meanwhile, the alternative version has Owen sporting rather flashy gold boots with a red trim. I can offer no explanation why this might have arisen, and can only attribute it to a factory change.

We travel to Japan for our next variant, as in Miniatures Series 12 we have Cristiano Ronaldo in Manchester United home kit MC5808. The image created by Corinthian has Ronaldo wearing red boots – the more common version – but is an alternative with CR7 wearing white boots, notoriously tricky for collectors to find.

Our final variant takes us across two continents and involves Gianluca Zambrotta in Barcelona home kit MC9309. He was initially released in German Series 3 in 2006 wearing black boots, and then in 2007 he was included in the Brazilian *Craques da Bola* Series, which saw the Italian wearing gold boots. I can only assume it was a factory change which resulted in them being painted gold.

Collectors Left Chasing Keys

Corinthian produced a series of MicroStars Key Rings exclusively for the Japanese market, with the series featuring some of the top names in football, and all players held in high esteem by fans in Japan.

National heroes Shunsuke Nakamura and Hidetoshi Nakata are joined by idol Roberto Baggio, along with Ronaldinho, Deco, Luis Figo, Manuel Rui Costa and Alessandro Del Piero.

There are 22 figures to collect in all, the figures being released in blind boxes in the same style as the Miniatures series of MicroStars. You were never sure which figure you would receive, with 15 blind boxes in each CDU. The series was released in 2007 and was incredibly well received in Japan, which was no great surprise given the incredible line-up. The figures have remained largely elusive for most collectors, with some proving practically impossible to find.

Fourteen of these figures were also released as a Phone Strap, the figures being identical except with a strap replacing the the key chain. Just to keep us on our toes, however, eight figures remained exclusive to the key ring style, and this is the source of the greater rarities. We have Shunsuke Nakamura in the away kits of Celtic and Reggina, Hidetoshi Nakata in away kits for Bolton Wanderers and Fiorentina, Roberto Baggio in away kits for Italy and Juventus, and Deco and Ronaldinho in Barcelona away kit.

The Nakata in Fiorentina away kit was the very last

Corinthian figure Lennart Van de Winkel needed to complete his entire collection, and it had long eluded him. On a routine search of Japanese auction sites, Lennart's heart jumped as he saw an auction containing the Nakata Fiorentina away kit key ring. Lennart enlisted the aid of a Japanese friend to secure the purchase, with the figure being hand delivered to him, a very proud moment.

This series also held my last figures, as I was chasing the final two key rings, Nakamura Celtic away and Baggio Italy away. My good friend Wee Jirasakul was able to find these for sale in Thailand, a truly amazing feeling to finally complete the collection.

The Legend of the Cancelled Series

Miniatures Series 10 was by all accounts the best selling series of Miniatures to date, so it was widely expected that a second series of Legends would be made – and eventually the rumours were proven true as details began to emerge. What could possibly go wrong now?

A full list of who was to be included appeared on the fabulous 'CorinthianSeller' website, and the names on there really whet collectors' appetites. The provisional list comprised of 28 players, eight of which would get released as part of Germany Series 3 wave two, namely Jurgen Klinsmann, Karl-Heinz Rummenigge, Frank Rijkaard, Marco Van Basten, Gary Lineker, Michel Platini, Gabriel Batistuta and Dino Zoff.

But what of the other 20? Well, there was a trio from AC Milan: George Weah and Zvonimir Boban in away kit along with goalkeeper Sebastiano Rossi. Neighbours Inter were represented by a German trio in Matthias Sammer and Andrea Brehme in home kit and Lothar Matthäus in away kit, along with Giuseppe Bergomi in home kit.

There was a host of figures from Italy's Series A in home kit: for Parma there is Faustino Asprilla and Lazio has Roberto Mancini, then Dunga for Fiorentina, Ruud Gullit for Sampdoria, Didier Deschamps for Juventus and Josep Guardiola for Brescia.

A Barcelona duo of Michael Laudrup and Hristo Stoichkov wore home kit, likewise Marc Overmars for Arsenal, and completing the series would have been Hidetoshi Nakata in Fiorentina home and away kit, joined by fellow countryman Shunsuke Nakamura in the home and away kits of Reggina.

There was never any official reason given as to why this series was cancelled. It may have been related to the marked decline in Corinthian collecting in Japan by this stage that saw the range deemed not commercially viable. The last few Miniatures were essentially just a repackaged product, with a relatively low cost in comparison to creating what would have been an entirely new and unique series, requiring multiple new sculpts.

Most of these unreleased Master Models were sold off by Corinthian, a lot went to Madbooth in Japan, and it's a real shame we never got what would have been first-time MicroStars releases of players like Asprilla, Rossi, Boban and Brehme.

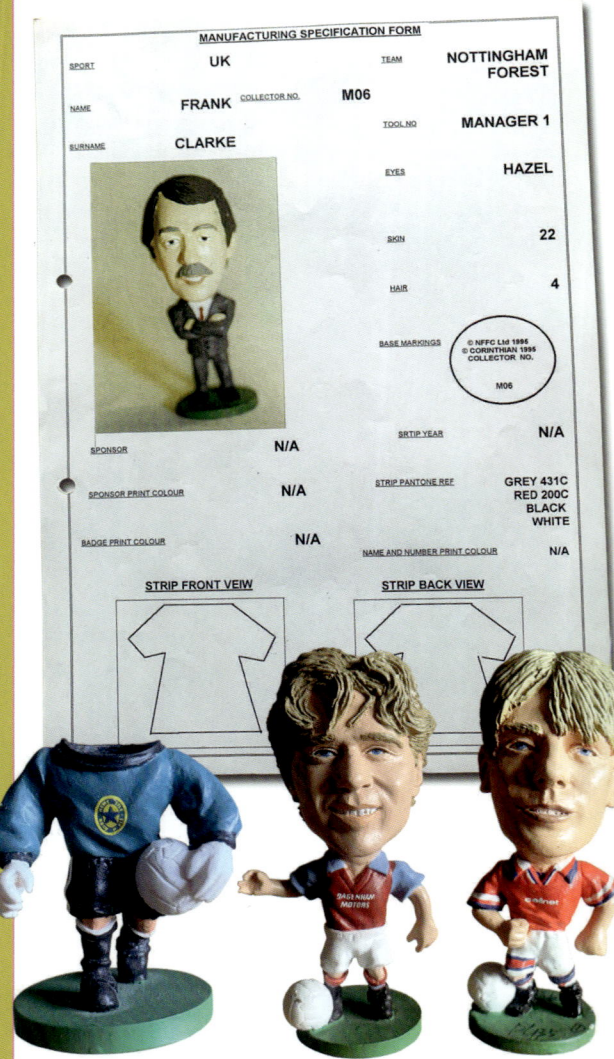

Production Sheets Are Saved

Something that has always fascinated collectors is the process involved in creating and manufacturing Corinthian's famous football figures.

Corinthian themselves did give a brief detailing of the production line in their *1999 Collectors Yearbook,* and there were also model makers present at the Conventions at Villa Park where you could observe the sculpting process in person. There's always been a clamour from collectors to get their hands on pieces of Corinthian ephemera but unfortunately there is a real dearth of material available.

Personally, I'm vastly fortunate to have in my collection a folder filled with original Corinthian production sheets, which detail all the information the factory would need to manufacture the figure, including colours to use, shirt number and base-stamp details.

I have production sheets for some of the rarest figures produced, such as Kennet Andersson and Juan Carlos Ablanedo, along with some for unreleased figures, and I simply had to include one in this book. My selection is a Master that precious few people have ever seen, Southampton goalkeeper Dave Beasant.

As you can see, he was assigned a collector code of PL257 and was all set for release for Southampton. I assume his release was put on hold due to his loan move to Nottingham Forest, where, in turn, he would fail to get a release due to the club's relegation from the Premier League in the 1996/97 season.

Corinthian would have a production sheet for every figure they planned on releasing, at least during the

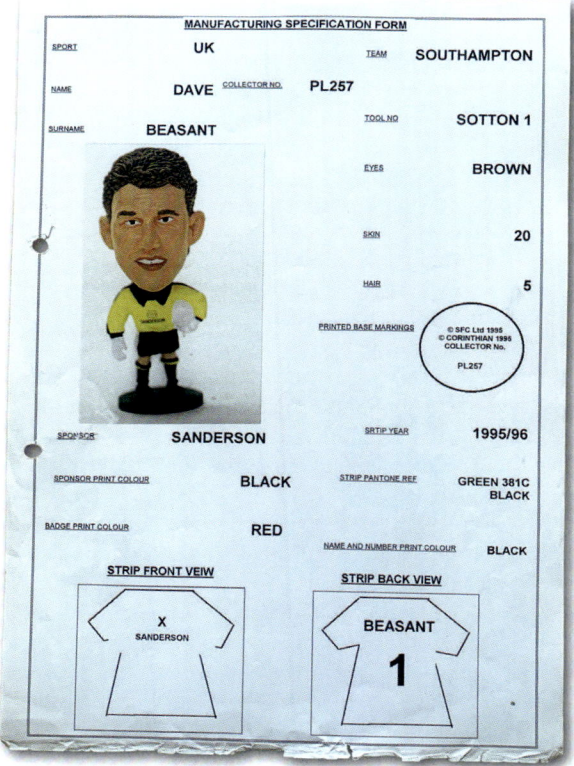

time of the Headliners figures, 1995 through to 1998. In my folder I have 50 production sheets, three of which are for unreleased figures. This is only a small percentage of the total number of figures Corinthian actually released. I really hope more of these sheets have survived, as they provide a fascinating historical glimpse 'behind the scenes'.

Legend of the Great Dane

Perhaps one of the most frequent questions I'm asked about the Corinthian figures is, "whatever happened to Peter Schmeichel?"

The collector's information file that came with the FAPL Collection figures shows a Peter Schmeichel for Manchester United in a unique body pose, where the goalkeeper is cupping the football in his hands, about to kick it.

The image used is of the Master Model, which were often used by Corinthian for promotional material, due to the time taken to produce the actual figure. So what could have happened to this Master, and why did it fail to appear?

Well, let's start with the reason for its cancellation and why that particular body pose was never used by Corinthian. The main concern was how stable the figure would be, with concerns that due to the pose the figure would be 'top heavy' and prone to falling over. To add some weight to this theory, let me explain what actually happened to the Master Model, and how it was found over 15 years after its creation, as Corinthian themselves had never auctioned it off.

Sadly, Corinthian went into administration, and as a result the remaining Headliners and ProStars Master Models were sold to one particular collector. It was then my job, if you can even call it that, to help him sell the

Master Models and find them deserving new homes.

During a phone call to discuss how sales were progressing, he informed me that Corinthian had been doing some sorting in the offices and had stumbled across a box of broken Master Models, and posted them on as part of the bulk deal. While on the phone, he sent me an email with photos of the broken Master Models attached – and as I scrolled through the photos, my heart stopped. There it was. After all these long years, it had been found: the Peter Schmeichel in kick pose Master Model.

I was left speechless. Something which for over 15 years was assumed to have been lost or destroyed was found. The Master Model was broken at the left ankle and, as a result, was no longer attached to the base. Furthermore, it was also broken at the neck: now, was this breakage responsible for Corinthian's decision to reconsider the pose's viability? We'll never know the answer; but, either way, it was consigned to the broken box and passed out of all memory.

The Master Model remained in my personal collection for

NICKY BUTT
Collector No.
PL281

PETER SCHMEICHEL
Collector No.
PL81

DENNIS IRWIN
Collector No.
PL101

PAUL PARKER
Collector No.
PL121

some time, taking pride of place, until an offer came in that even I was unable to refuse. Of course, I lament the sale of the truly legendary Schmeichel in kick pose, however at that time the money being offered was simply eye-watering and couldn't be refused. I take solace in the fact that he now resides with a truly deserving collector, and would never have sold him otherwise.

I've included the photo I was originally sent of Schmeichel on that fateful night when he was found, along with a picture taken when he was part of my personal Master Model collection, so you can see this incredible model in full. Had Corinthian released this ill-fated figure, then there's no doubt it would have been one of the most popular of all.

The Myth of the Raincoat

For years there was a long-standing rumour, a myth if you will, regarding a mysterious Master Model that some collectors and traders claimed to have seen; but but very little information was forthcoming, beyond the fact that he was wearing a raincoat...

The night that I saw and acquired the kick pose Master Model of Peter Schmeichel was the very same night that this myth turned into reality. During the phone conversation when I was sent images of various broken Master Models, my friend said, "Okay, that's everything – apart from this old bloke in a raincoat!"

I immediately requested a photo and, there he was. Harry Vermeegen.

Now, I understand the name will probably mean nothing to you, so allow me to provide some context. Harry Vermeegan was a recording artiste and actor as well as a TV personality who presented a Dutch football show called *De Regenjas*, which in English is – yes, you guessed it, 'The Raincoat'.

As yet a further string to his bow, Harry was also the promoter of the Corinthian figures in the Netherlands. On the Dutch Lottery TV show he gave away free figures to participants, and his face appeared on some promotional items.

Lennart Van de Winkel once had a sit-down interview with someone who worked on the range and, during the conversation, he was browsing through his Corinthian files. When Lennart glimpsed the words 'Commentator figurine', he exclaimed, "Please go back." And then he saw it... 'HARRY VERMEEGEN'. It included pictures of the sculpt, of Harry himself, and a note: 'WILL NOT BE RELEASED'.

Lennart was told the figure was never made available because of the raincoat; there was no exact reason stated, but it certainly had to do with that coat. The intention was to release Vermeegen as part of the Dutch *De Spelers Colectie* range of Eredivisie players, possibly as a redemption-style figure. We'll never now know the exact plan, or why he was pulled.

For 15 years, the Harry Vermeegen unreleased Master Model resided with Corinthian, lost and forgotten; but now he proudly sits in my Master Model cabinet and is possibly the favourite example of all those I own – besides Ruel Fox, of course.

Emerson Sambas into My Collection

The story of how the incredible unreleased Master Model of Emerson came to be in my collection starts in Bolton, of all places.

As we know, there were only four Corinthian figures released as part of the FAPL Collection; but there were plenty more sculpted and intended for release. I actually have more unreleased Bolton Wanderers masters in my collection than officially Corinthian-released figures, all of them having been cancelled after the Trotters' relegation from the Premiership in the 1995/96 season.

On a routine eBay search, the item at the top of the page was an unreleased Master Model of Mixu Paatelainen for Bolton. Surprisingly, he was up for a 'Buy It Now' price of just £110. So I snapped him up in a moment, not believing my luck.

I contacted the seller to see if there were any more Master Models available, and he told me that he and his brother had both purchased a Master Model at a live Corinthian auction, and

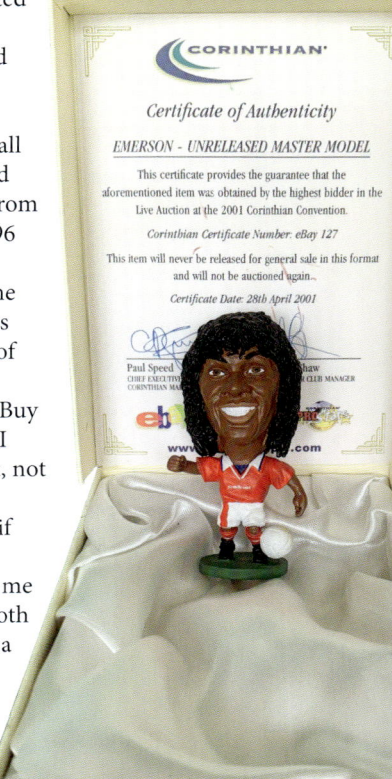

that he would get back in touch with me if the other one might be available.

A few hours later I received a call back: his brother did still have his Master Model up in his loft, and he'd be happy to sell it for the same price I paid for Mixu. The photo was attached, and my jaw hit the floor when I saw the Master Model was none other than Emerson.

Swiftly, I completed the purchase and a few days later the parcel arrived. I was still hardly convinced it could be real, until I opened the Master Model box and there he was – the broad beaming smile of Brazilian midfielder Emerson. It's a truly magnificent sculpt, and such a shame Corinthian never got to release this figure. His master is without doubt the one I receive the most enquiries about, and to date the highest offer I have turned down is £2,500. He is simply not for sale at any price, and stands in my Master Model display cabinet next to the unreleased manager sculpt of Bryan Robson.

*Available 1997... We're Still Waiting

On the back of the FAPL Collection blister packs for the 1996/97 range was an information box detailing the full range of teams available, with three teams having an asterix* next to their name.

'* Teams marked with an asterix available 1997', the footnote promised, the three teams being the newly promoted trio of Derby County, Leicester City and Sunderland. Well, it's now 2025, and we're still waiting.

To the best of my knowledge, Corinthian had eight sculpts made for Derby County: Dean Sturridge, Igor Štimac, Chris Powell, Marco Gabbiadini, Paul Simpson, Sean Flynn, Robbie van der Laan, and they even auctioned off a repaint of Paul Parker. There are some truly amazing sculpts amongst them, the Dean Sturridge being part

of my personal collection, acquired from the infamous broken Master Model box at Corinthian, and he was recently joined by Gabbiadini.

As for Leicester City, so far five have been seen, namely Mark Robins, Garry Parker, Simon Grayson, Jimmy Willis and the superb sculpt of Jamie Lawrence and his vertical dreadlocks. We were truly robbed not getting this exceptional figure released.

On to Sunderland now, who also had five figures sculpted: Tony Coton, Paul Bracewell, Niall Quinn, Michael Gray and Richard Ord. Perhaps, as a Newcastle United supporter, I shouldn't be admitting that I have four of those in my personal collection. It's a classic case of my Corinthian heart overruling my club allegiance. The only one that evades me is Richard Ord,

By this point it was late 1996, and it was becoming ever clearer to Corinthian that their best-selling figures were, predictably, top stars and the top teams, hence the decision was taken that it wouldn't be commercially viable to produce figures from these three new teams. Did Corinthian sculpt even more than I've detailed here? Well, it's highly probable.

A Mid-size Mystery

In the early part of 2000, an image appeared online of some very interesting and unique Corinthian figures. To this day, no one is entirely sure of the source of the photograph, and its contents have never been explained or even mentioned by Corinthian.

The photo was of some Corinthian Master Models and blank, unpainted plastic figures; but these were mid-size figures, taller than a MicroStars but smaller than a ProStars.

A few theories have been suggested. Perhaps they were produced as a size sample for what would evolve into MicroStars? This idea has always carried the most weight with me. Given the players involved and the timeframe when the photo surfaced, it would fit in with the development of MicroStars. There's not too much difference sizewise between these mystery figures and the ProStars, so it is plausible Corinthian decided to scale down

even further. The packaging also needs to be factored in, and these simply wouldn't fit inside a PowerPodz capsule.

A theory was floated that perhaps the figures represented an entirely new venture, where Corinthian were planning to release a 'paint-it-yourself' range. I personally love that idea but I don't feel it's correct, more likely just suggested by the fact that four of the figures are blank and unpainted.

So who are the figures? Of course, we have David Beckham for Manchester United and also in an England away kit; there's also Ryan Giggs for Manchester United, along with Jaap Stam and his unpainted figure. Dennis Bergkamp and David Seaman appear for Arsenal, and for north London rivals Tottenham Hotspur there's David Ginola in both painted and unpainted forms.

The Chelsea duo are Tore Andre Flo and Gustavo Poyet, with Poyet also having an unpainted figure; there's Titi Camara for Liverpool, Michael Owen for England, Dion Dublin for Aston Villa, Harry Kewell for Leeds United, Lorenzo Amoruso for Rangers, the excellent Paolo Di Canio for West Ham United and Christian Ziege for Middlesbrough.

In my personal collection I have the Ziege painted Master Model, along with the three unpainted figures of Stam, Ginola and Poyet.

As for the rest, I have absolutely no clue what happened to them or where they are now, but hopefully they're all still intact and part of a collection somewhere, proudly on display.

The Time Has Come

I've saved something very special to close the book – something that I've known about for a number of years but have only shown to a few collectors. But now the time has come to reveal... the Corinthian Clock!

Corinthian produced a superb sales representative brochure that contained details and images of the full range of Corinthian products, including pack sizes and trade prices, and one of the pages showcases the Headliners England Alarm Clock.

This would have been a fully functioning FM/AM radio alarm clock designed around a goalmouth/stadium scenario, with an electronic scoreboard LCD display, and the bucket and sponge acting as the volume control. The alarm featured real football crowd noise, and was turned off by using the player to 'kick' and score a goal.

It gets even better. There was even a roof display stand area to hold up to nine figures, the base being embossed with the 'HEADLINERS' logo, a goal with crowd backing display and even two corner posts with flags.

The information sheet states three players would have been included, and shows Beckham and Shearer in England 1998 kit along with goalkeeper Stefan Klos for Borussia Dortmund. The trade price is listed as £15.31, so it would have retailed at around £35 on its expected release date... of July 1998.

I can envisage myself waking up every morning for school to the crowd noise, and having Ruel Fox score past Peter Schmeichel to turn my alarm off. This exceptional product really would have to be the Holy Grail for any Corinthian

ENGLAND

A full function radio alarm clock with electronic scoreboard LCD display, snooze button, FM / AM radio bands, and volume control via the bucket and sponge on the pitch. The alarm features real football crowd noise with demo button which switches off by using the player to 'kick' and score a goal. (3 players included).
The stadium roof display stand area also holds up to 9 Headliners figures (not supplied) and the product comes packaged in an acetate fronted box with full details and visuals of the product on the back and sides of the box. The radio alarm is battery operated and comes complete with full instructions.

CORINTHIAN HEADLINERS

PRODUCT
ELECTRONIC RADIO ALARM CLOCK

PIECE REFERENCE
ENG1019

PIECE BARCODE
5029310790192

PIECE PRICE
£15.31

PACK QUANTITY
4

AVAILABILITY
JULY 1998

collector to own, if indeed it still exists. Will I ever own this lost piece of Corinthian history? Only time will tell.

AUTHOR

Craig was born and raised in Scunthorpe, North Lincolnshire, however he didn't grow up a Scunthorpe fan, nor did he follow his dad and brother in supporting Tottenham Hotspur, opting instead for Newcastle United, due to a certain Ruel Fox. Years of mediocrity and misery followed until, in 2025, the Toon won the Carabao Cup! He has collected Corinthians for over 30 years, amassing a collection of over 10,000 figures, along with creating the Corinthian Archive website.

ACKNOWLEDGMENTS

To my Mum and Dad, who shared my passion for collecting and encouraged it, buying me figures for every birthday and Christmas; my brother Glenn who I began the collecting journey with, and my little sister Cheryl for always being there to listen to my excitement when I found a figure I'd been searching for. Lennart Van de Winkel for experiencing this collector's journey with me; Davide Ravinale for sharing my passion for collecting; Dave Rule for being the undisputed king of Corinthian selling; the 'Old Skool' collectors, Jim Pinder and Johnny Carson, who were always so gracious with their time; and Laura Trocaru for always believing in me, thank you Muffin. The final person to thank is my Nanna, who always supported my collection, both emotionally and financially.

COLLECTOR HALL OF FAME

Thanks to everyone who ordered the book in advance.

Anthony Lewins | Christopher McColgan | Adam Bell
Philip & James Brunskill | Charlie Robery | Stuart Reilly
Blain Hoskins | Connor Hoskins | Liam Maden
CRMG Corinthians | Tim Griffiths | Alan Coyle
Stuart Oxton | Maikel Rozijn | Stephen Gorman
Dan Smail | Greg Baker | Christopher Perrett | Mark Hall
Duncan Leatherdale | Mike Dunlop | Stephen Martin
Matthew Lovekin | Ökkes Çürük jr | Mark Krzeczunowicz
Jonathon Buck | Kevin Worboys | James Gordon
David Miller | Dan Taborda | Chris Wells | Cheryl Robinson
Kevin McKnight | Michael 'Eddie' Bishop | Wayne Colegate
Jon Lovelock | Jonathan Cater | Stephen Robson
James Taylor | Craig Jackson | Sean Kinsella | Gary Galbraith
Ashley Wren | Phil Everett | Richard Leatherdale
Chris Whitehead | Marc Morris | Adam Bates | Adam Ball
Craig Nutt | Stephen Marriott | Adam Hartles | Sam Rearden
Rob Stokes | Craig Smith | Greg Ross | Jonathan Keight
Rob Soper | Leandro Gaspar | Jos Rasenberg | Ryan Dixon
Andrew Schofield | Goh Chin Leng | Nigel Neo
Desmond Koh | Brian Wen | Lennart Van de Winkel
Nye Rees | Peter Timothy | Clive Collard | Harvey Collins
Aaron Enrique Perez | Richard Maddy | Rishi Gathrie
Ong-Art Natheemat | Wee Jirasakul | David Cook
Alvin Koh | Sonny Whitelock | Niphot Krailas-olarn
Ian Miller | Gerrit Oldekamp | Tanat Boonthanapat
Jos Slovick | Graham Joseph | Liam Raby | Alex Sharp

Jesper Nöteberg | Yingsak Boonchamnan
Paul Steele | Agung Budi Setiyanto
Surachest Phornsuwannapha | Damien Orchard
William Carruthers | James Hart | Andrew Flack
Martin Anthony Walters | David Rule
Andrew Bragg | Ryan Gibson | Jeremy Bijl
Gareth Segovia-Thomas | Lucy Ennis-Sewell
Jeroen van der Jagt | Hien Nguyen Huu
Alan Witts | Emma Frear | Kai Evans
Jamie Millar | Stuart Voss | Massimo Scavello
Steve Yau | Philip Caspell | Jamie Winters
Mark Wilcox | Henry Mills | Davide Mirarchi
Alistair Rea | Craig Jeff | Phongsiri Salee
Karl Seed | Mark Saunders | Gary Brown | David Fleming
Stuart Albon | Tim Lawrence | Austin Dawkins | Hiro A
Olly Rafferty Arsenal Collector @ THEARSENAL1886
Martin Grocott | Wayne Pepper | Mark van der Haar
Roshdi Nasir | Daryl Thomas | Jon McGinn | Janson Tidy
Chris Baggaley | Chance Bowen | Mark Beagan
Emze | Sam Case | Gregg Dubner | M Wilmot | Zolt Veres
Derek Taylor | Davide Ravinale | Andrew Armstrong
Ivan Raby | Victor Torres | Matt Carnelley | Mark Balfe
Jeff Sutherland (corinthians_afc) | Tony Sharpe
Steve 'Scruffy the Janitor' Swain | Darren Courtney
Chris Guerin | Paul W Fargher | Timo Tschöpel
Arthur & Alfie Warrington | Mrs Muffin | Rikky Smith
David Silman & Jonathan Silman | Martin Hamilton
Jeff Salmond & Tim Salmond | Grayson Sarath
Jake Adlington @ Corinthian MicroStars | Colin McLeish

Jonathan Hughes | Zhou Tianhang | Alex Large
Tom McIver | Lars Engelhard | Gary Heffer | Dave Phelan
William Yau | Christopher Sommerville | Neil Halton
Neil McNerlan | Sam Clark | Chris Knowles | Woody
Luke Fitch | Jason Monks | Catherine Bibby | Adam Diouri
Adam Newland | Rich Barlow - Sheffield | Robert Murphy
Argyris Saridis | Stratos Tsoynis | Lampros Apostolidis
Marios Galanis | Big Bear & Pal | Dave & Lynne Welch
Peter Checkley | Glenn Robinson | Darren Welch
Frank Newton | Colin Shaw | Thomas Shaw | Daniel Shaw
Philip Boardman | Alonso Wong | Steve Chan | Matt Gunn
Stephen Dalling | Johnathan Rudland | Ben Chamberlain
James 'Djismi' Shorten | Sunil Chapanery | Ian Wilkinson
Jake Buckley | Chris Griffiths | Andrew Noble
Alexander Werpachowski | Bobbo Jørgen Langeland
David Johnson | Tinarom Yamprasert | Andy Raybould
Dave Downes (Instagram's @oldboyfootballshirts)
Sivakumaar, Yeo WH, Nicholas Phua & Rex - Singapore